'Green' Taxes and Charges: Policy and Practice in Britain and Germany

Stephen Smith

The Institute for Fiscal Studies
7 Ridgmount Street
London WC1E 7AÉ

Thi

Published by
The Institute for Fiscal Studies
7 Ridgmount Street
London WC1E 7AE
tel. (44) 171 636 3784
fax (44) 171 323 4780

Printed by
KKS Printing
Stanway Street
London N1 6RZ

Preface

This report is based on research at the Institute for Fiscal Studies in London, UK, supported by the Anglo German Foundation for the Study of Industrial Society; this research has been undertaken in collaboration with the Institut für Angewandte Wirtschaftsforschung in Tübingen, Germany. The author is grateful to the Foundation for this financial support, and to the officers of the Foundation for their advice and encouragement.

In addition, the IFS programme of research on tax policy and the environment has received financial support from the UK Economic and Social Research Council through ESRC Research Centre funding for IFS, from the European Commission's Environment Programme, from a consortium of companies, and from the Esmée Fairbairn Charitable Trust. Various parts of this report draw on research co-funded by these sponsors.

The author wishes to acknowledge the contribution to the research programme made by researchers at Tübingen, especially Uwe Hochmuth. In addition, the report draws on IFS research that the author has undertaken jointly with other IFS staff, including Laura Blow, Ian Crawford, Mark Pearson and Najma Rajah, and he is happy to acknowledge their considerable contribution to the work reported here.

UK Family Expenditure Survey data are used in Chapters 4, 6 and 7 by permission of the Central Statistical Office. The UK Simulation Programme for Indirect Taxes used in Chapter 6 has been developed by a number of IFS staff and research associates, including Paul Baker, James Banks, Richard Blundell, Ian Crawford, Panos Pashardes, Elizabeth Symons and Ian Walker. The manuscript has been prepared for publication by Judith Payne.

The views expressed in this report are those of the author alone, and not those of the Anglo German Foundation or other sponsors, nor of the Institute for Fiscal Studies, which has no corporate views.

Stephen Smith is Deputy Director of the Institute for Fiscal Studies and Reader in Economics at University College London.

Contents

tion of economic instruments including environmental taxes and charges. The Green Party's position in this document was that taxes should supplement rather than replace a strict regulatory system. Environmental tax proposals included the introduction of an air emissions charge, a primary energy tax, substantial mineral oil tax increases, the introduction of an HGV charge, a modification of the vehicle excise duty (VED) base to replace cylinder capacity with environmental attributes, the introduction of a waste deposit charge, a packaging charge, a basic chemicals charge, a pesticides and fertiliser charge, water extraction and waste water charges, and land-use charge on impermeable coverings to the land surface (Jüttner, 1990).

Political pressure from the rise of the Greens has been felt most acutely by the Social Democratic Party (SPD), and amongst the established parties, the SPD developed the first, and most extensive, proposals for environmental taxes. The possibility of using environmental charges/taxes was first raised in the 'Nuremburg Programme for Action' (Nürnberger Aktionsprogramm) of 1986. More detailed proposals including product, energy and air emissions charges were passed by the party congress in Münster in 1988, laying the ground for the party's main policy review for the 1990s and the 1990 general election, known as 'Progress '90' (Fortschritt '90) which ambitiously set out the transformation of the German economy into an 'environmental and social market economy'. The party's specific proposals focused primarily on the introduction of an energy tax, the revenues of which were to be used to finance the abolition of VED, a series of transfers within the income tax and social security system to compensate for the regressive effect of the tax, and investment incentives to accelerate and facilitate structural reform. In addition, charges were proposed for disposable beverage containers, air emissions, special waste, waste water and intensive livestock farming.

Despite this substantial catalogue of comprehensive proposals, and the vigorous debate during the late 1980s, only a limited number of environmental tax measures have in practice been introduced.[2] German reunification has brought with it new policy concerns and new economic priorities, and the willingness of German policymakers and the German public to pursue a stringent policy of environmental protection has been increasingly tempered by concern about its potential economic costs. Within the European Community, Germany no longer stands out as the leading advocate of major new environmental policy measures; there have, for example, been clear German reservations about the wisdom, cost-effectiveness and political acceptability of the proposed EC carbon tax.

In the UK, widespread policy awareness of environmental issues did not develop until the start of the 1990s. The initial impetus came from an extraordinary level of voter support in the 1989 European Parliament elections for the Green Party, which had previously achieved little either in the way of votes or public profile in UK elections. Although, under the system of voting used in the UK, the Green Party did not secure a single seat, its share of the vote eclipsed the support of the centre party, the Liberal Democrats, and appeared to establish the Green Party as a significant force in UK politics.

In the event, the political support enjoyed by the Green Party disappeared after the European Parliament elections almost as quickly as it had materialised. Nevertheless, the response of the established political parties, and especially of the government, sharply increased the profile of environmental issues in UK politics for a considerably longer period.

---

[2] Umweltbundesamt (1994) provides a recent overview of the environmental taxes and charges employed in Germany.

Shortly after the European Parliament elections, the then Prime Minister, Margaret Thatcher, announced that higher priority was to be given to environmental issues throughout government. A major review of government environmental policy followed, culminating in a White Paper, *This Common Inheritance: Britain's Environmental Strategy* (HMSO, 1990). This paper began with a ringing declaration of a shift in government attitudes:

> There are moments in history when apparently disparate forces or issues come together and take shape. Almost half a century ago that was true of arguments about the welfare state. In the last decade, the case for market economics has emerged, coherent and formidable, as a blueprint for prosperity and a guarantee of freedom. Today it is the environment that captures headlines and excites public opinion.
> (HMSO, 1990, p. 8)

One distinctive innovation in the 1990 White Paper was an annex setting out the scope for using market instruments in environmental protection. A year earlier, extended use of such instruments had been advocated in an influential report written for the Department of the Environment (Pearce, Markandya and Barbier, 1989). Although the intellectual case for greater use of market instruments had been long established in theory, and had been picked up by policy tracts written from both ends of the political spectrum (Ridley, 1989; Owens, Anderson and Brunskill, 1990), this was the first occasion that a commitment had been made to review the scope for their application over the whole spectrum of government policies and activities.

As in Germany, actual policy developments have been slow in forthcoming. To date, the only tax measures implemented with a primary rationale in terms of their environmental effects have been changes to the tax differentials between motor fuels; plans for another measure —

the landfill levy — are, however, now well advanced. Other tax measures that have been at least partly justified in environmental terms have been a little more substantial. Two measures undertaken primarily with revenue interests in mind have also been justified in terms of their potential environmental benefits, especially in terms of reductions in the UK's greenhouse gas emissions: the government has committed itself to a steady 3 per cent annual increase in motor fuel duties in real terms over coming years, and introduced value added tax on domestic energy from April 1994. Beyond these measures actually implemented, other initiatives based on market mechanisms and taxation are under active consideration, including some form of road-use charging (although again primarily intended to raise revenues) and the possibility of some form of market mechanism covering sulphur emissions.

More so than Germany, the UK government has been strongly opposed to the development of environmental tax policies at the level of the European Community. At an ECOFIN meeting held in the middle of 1992, the UK was the only member state to state unequivocal opposition to the European Commission's proposal for a European carbon tax. Whilst economic concerns, especially about the impact of the tax on industrial competitiveness in trade with non-member states, may have been part of the reason for the UK's opposition, it has also been consistent with the UK's long-standing unwillingness to see any expansion of the EC's involvement in tax policy.

1.2 Structure of this Report

Against this background of limited current and prospective tax policy measures for environmental reasons, this report aims to take stock of what British and German policies have achieved to date, and of the scope for more extensive use of 'green' charging and taxation.

6

The report begins in Chapters 2 and 3 by setting out a framework for assessing the potential contribution that taxes and charges could make to environmental management. What, in principle, might be achieved by using taxes and charges that could not be done equally well by regulatory policies or other 'conventional' measures? In what contexts might taxes and charges be most likely to improve the working of environmental policy, and how should they be designed to maximise the benefits from their use?

In Chapters 4 to 7, the report turns to consideration of environmental taxes and charges in four key fields of environmental policy, relating to water, waste, energy and transport, respectively. In each chapter, the aim is twofold:

- first, to describe, and compare, the uses made of taxes and charges to date in the environmental policies of both Britain and Germany, in each of the four fields;
- second, drawing on both theoretical considerations and the experience accumulated in the two countries to date, to indicate where British policy could go further, either by introducing new environmental taxes and charges or by modifying existing instruments to enhance their environmental effectiveness.

CHAPTER 2
The Case for 'Market Mechanisms' in Environmental Policy[3]

The need for public intervention to control environmental pollution arises because of the 'externalities' involved in pollution — the costs that the polluting individual or firm imposes on other members of society. Without government intervention, a polluter may have no reason to take these external costs into account. Decisions about the level of production and consumption activities that give rise to pollution, about the choice of technology, the use of pollution-abatement measures and the disposal of waste products will then all be taken purely on the basis of the 'private' costs and benefits to the individual polluter. In particular, the atmosphere and water systems may be treated as free methods for disposing of unwanted waste products, despite the fact that unrestricted pollution of the atmosphere, or of groundwater, rivers and seas, may impose costs on other firms or individuals.

Environmental policy needs to draw a balance between the costs of pollution and the costs of controlling pollution. Whilst there may be some forms of pollution that it would be desirable to eliminate entirely, this will generally be the exception rather than the rule. Ideally, pollution should be restricted up to the point where the benefits to society as a whole from further reductions in pollution are less than the costs of controlling pollution through the installation of control devices or the curtailment of polluting activities. In economic terms, therefore, pollution should be controlled up to the point where the marginal cost of further

---

[3]This chapter and Chapter 3 draw extensively on Smith (1992a).

abatement measures just outweighs the gain from reduced emissions.

For a single polluting firm (for example, a firm discharging organic matter into a river), we can draw marginal abatement cost (MAC) and marginal damage cost (MDC) functions as shown in Figure 2.1. The marginal abatement cost will generally rise (strictly will not fall) with more stringent control, since the MAC curve assumes a ranking of measures, such that the least costly are implemented first. Often, too, the marginal damage cost will rise with emissions, reflecting a tendency for large amounts of pollution to cause proportionately greater damage to the environment than small amounts of pollution. This might be the case if the environment has some natural assimilative capacity — as in the case of the ability of water systems to assimilate organic matter. In the diagram, E^* represents the efficient level of pollution control. At E^*, the marginal abatement cost and marginal damage cost are equal, at a level C^*.

In theoretical terms, the appropriate level of abatement is achieved where the marginal social cost of reducing pollution by an additional unit is equal to the marginal

FIGURE 2.1

Efficient pollution abatement for a single polluting firm

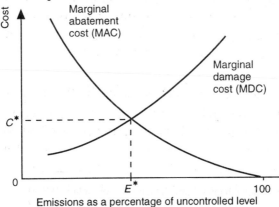

Emissions as a percentage of uncontrolled level

social benefit of a one-unit reduction in pollution. Achieving this level, whether through tax policies or through other measures, requires information on the structure of both marginal abatement costs and marginal damage costs. As the survey by Cropper and Oates (1992) shows, considerable progress has been made in recent years in refining the methods for obtaining the information needed to determine the optimal level of pollution abatement. Extensive research has, for example, been undertaken into the valuation of marginal environmental improvements, using both indirect inference from the market prices of housing and other commodities affected by environmental conditions, and direct survey evidence ('contingent valuation') of the values that individuals place on environmental improvements.

In practice, the context for many environmental policy decisions is already more tightly defined than in the above analysis of 'optimal' pollution control. Many countries have already undertaken quantitative commitments to reduce greenhouse gas emissions, for example, and may wish to use environmental taxes to achieve these targets. In these circumstances, the main issue concerns the scale of the response to tax changes, in terms of the price elasticity of demand for the taxed products. Although there may be considerable uncertainty about the magnitude of these elasticities, measures can always be implemented on a gradual basis, increasing tax rates until the desired quantitative response is achieved.

2.1 Advantages of Market Mechanisms

In principle, any given pattern of pollution reduction could be achieved either by 'command-and-control' regulations, restricting emissions to a given level, or by use of market mechanisms such as pollution taxes and charges, to provide an appropriate incentive to reduce emissions to the same level. Thus, in Figure 2.1, a charge of C^* per unit of pollution could be used to reach the optimal level of emissions, E^*, or regulations could require the polluter to abate emissions to the same level. However, whilst charging mechanisms and regulations can be used to equivalent effect in the context of this simple example, in more complex situations, there may be some important gains from using market mechanisms such as emissions taxes instead of 'command-and-control' regulations.

- *Static cost minimisation.* The static efficiency gains from the use of market-based instruments arise in situations where polluters face different opportunities for pollution abatement or different marginal abatement costs. The costs of reducing polluting emissions may in practice vary between polluters for a variety of reasons. Different firms may use different technologies, some of which may be more able to accommodate reductions in polluting emissions than others. Similarly, the costs to individual households of reducing their use of particular polluting products may vary as a result of differences in tastes or individual circumstances. The efficient, cost-minimising, pattern of pollution abatement would require greater reductions in pollution by those polluters for whom the cost of each unit of pollution abatement was low, and would impose less stringent levels of abatement on polluters facing a high marginal cost of abatement.

  In theory, a fully-informed regulatory agency could tailor regulatory requirements to the circumstances of each polluter so as to achieve this outcome. However, it may in practice be unrealistic to expect regulatory agencies to have access to the kinds of information necessary to design the efficient allocation of abatement across polluters; much of the necessary information concerning relative abatement costs is in the hands of individual firms, which may not wish to reveal it to the regulator. Given these informational limitations on regulatory policy, it is more likely that regulatory rules will be applied uniformly to all polluters. Polluters with high abatement costs will be required to undertake as much abatement as those with lower costs, and pollution abatement will be more costly than the efficient minimum.

Market mechanisms have the attraction that they may induce polluters to choose the efficient, cost-minimising, pattern of abatement in response to the price signal they provide. A pollution tax, for example, that is imposed on each unit of emissions will mean that polluters with low abatement costs will be more likely to choose to abate, and to make larger reductions in emissions, than polluters for whom the costs of abatement are high. Polluters with low abatement costs will, in effect, volunteer to contribute higher levels of abatement, because the emissions tax makes additional abatement profitable for them. Conversely, the tax puts an upper limit on the cost of any abatement that takes place: polluters for whom unit abatement costs exceed the potential tax saving will not find it worth while to undertake abatement measures.

Empirical studies of the costs of pollution abatement using different abatement rules, summarised by Tietenberg (1990), show that the gains from efficiently allocating emission reductions between polluters can be substantial. For example, in a study of the cost of achieving strict abatement standards for nitrogen oxide pollution in Baltimore, US, Krupnick (1986) shows that efficient abatement would involve about one-sixth of the cost of uniform reductions in pollution imposed using command-and-control regulation.

- *Dynamic incentives for innovation.* In addition to the potential static efficiency advantages of market mechanisms, they may also confer dynamic efficiency gains, by providing an incentive for research and development in pollution-abatement technologies. Even at the level of emissions that constitutes the current cost-minimising level, polluters will continue to face an incentive to look for further cost-effective ways of achieving emissions reductions; with an emissions tax, for example, this incentive arises because polluters pay the tax on any remaining units of pollution. There is thus a potential gain to be made from the development of new technologies that would allow the level of pollution to be reduced still further. Market mechanisms may thus hold out the possibility of a more rapid rate of development of pollution-control technologies than regulatory policies, which provide polluters with little incentive to do more than the minimum required to comply with regulatory requirements.

- *Vulnerability to regulatory failure.* Market instruments such as emissions taxation may be less exposed to the risk of regulatory 'failure' than certain forms of quantitative regulation. One important source of regulatory failure is the asymmetry of information between regulators and their subjects (Vickers and Yarrow, 1988). Where a substantial amount of information about the circumstances or characteristics of individual firms is required to implement a particular policy, the firms may be in a strong position to control the flow of information to the regulator in such a way as to significantly affect the way the policy is applied. Although there may be little difference between a uniform rule on emissions levels (e.g. one setting an upper limit to emissions) and an emissions tax in the amount of information required for administration and enforcement, a regulatory policy that sought to take more account of the circumstances of individual firms would be much more vulnerable to regulatory failure. The efficient allocation of emissions abatement between firms depends on the marginal costs of abatement to each firm, and this information can only be obtained by the regulator from the firms themselves.

13

- *Revenues.* Both the static and dynamic efficiency arguments apply to market mechanisms in general. A further potential benefit of using market-based environmental policies may arise where, as in the case of environmental taxes (or auctioned tradable permits), these raise revenues. In some circumstances, the revenues raised through environmental market mechanisms may constitute a second source of benefits (or a 'double dividend') from their use, over and above their impact on the environment. This double dividend would take the form of a reduction in the efficiency cost of raising tax revenues, in the sense that the revenues raised from the environmental market mechanism could be substituted for taxes that impose distortionary costs on the economy, thus reducing the net aggregate dead-weight loss from raising public revenues (Terkla, 1984). Recent papers have shown that the issues concerning existence of a double dividend are complex, and that the circumstances where a double dividend might arise are quite limited. Whilst the revenues raised through some market mechanisms may be of value, the case for introducing such instruments should be made primarily on the basis of the environmental policy arguments, not the potential contribution to public revenues.

Market mechanisms such as environmental taxes will not, however, be suitable for all pollution problems. In some cases, regulation will be preferable. Some limitations of market mechanisms include the following:

- *Uncertainty.* The extent to which environmental taxes lead to an improvement in the environment will depend on the responses made by individual polluters to the incentive signal that a tax provides. Whilst it may be possible to make an assessment of the likely impact of a given tax on pollution, a particular quantitative reduction in pollution cannot be guaranteed, especially where there is considerable uncertainty about the costs of the abatement options open to individual polluters. If these costs turn out to be higher than was anticipated at the time the tax was set, the amount of abatement is likely to be lower than expected; conversely, if polluters' abatement costs are in practice lower than anticipated, the tax might have a greater impact than expected on the level of pollution. Predictability in the environmental impact of policy measures may be particularly important in some situations — for example, where there are threshold effects in environmental damage, or where a country has made policy commitments to achieve particular targets. In these circumstances, regulations or market mechanisms such as tradable permits which guarantee a particular pollution level may be preferable to environmental tax measures. However, in other contexts, where achievement of a particular outcome is less critical, there may be advantages to using tax instruments, since they place a ceiling on abatement costs and thus limit the amount of economic damage that might be caused if abatement costs turn out to be much higher than originally forecast.

- *Non-uniform damage.* Where the *concentration* of pollution, either in particular localities or over certain time periods, is of importance, more complex forms of tax instrument will be needed than where the concentration of pollutant emissions is irrelevant.[4] A straightforward tax per unit of effluent discharge (or, more generally, pollutant emitted) would not discourage geographical or temporal concentrations of pollution, whilst at the same time it could mean that firms in areas

---

[4]Cases where the geographical concentration of pollution is of no concern at all are rare; the emission of carbon dioxide (and its impact on global warming) probably provides the only significant practical example.

where pollution was less damaging might be charged more than the value of the damage created. Where policy is, none the less, constrained to use only uniform taxes, there is then a straightforward trade-off between the efficiency gain from taking into account the diversity of abatement costs and the efficiency costs of inadequately differentiating between polluters with different marginal abatement benefits (Seskin, Anderson and Reid, 1983). A number of papers have considered the use of zoned taxes or other non-linear tax systems to reflect the fact that pollution in particular localities or at certain times causes greater damage (Tietenberg, 1978; Kolstad, 1987).

- *Distribution.*   Where taxes are used to discourage pollution, the distribution of the burden of the tax payments may be unevenly spread across taxpayers. In some cases, where behavioural responses to the tax are relatively small and high tax rates are levied, the burden of additional tax payments could be substantial and could significantly alter the distributional incidence of the tax system as a whole. Environmental taxes on 'necessities' in household budgets, for example, could have a regressive distributional incidence across income groups and could conflict with public policy objectives of equity.
- *Monopoly.*   A theoretical disadvantage of emissions taxes is that where polluters have monopoly power in the output market, imposition of a pollution tax may induce excessive reductions in output, below the socially optimal level; this effect may not arise with direct regulation (Buchanan, 1969). However, whilst this drawback of market mechanisms is a theoretical possibility, it appears that in practice its quantitative significance may be low (Oates and Strassmann, 1984).

CHAPTER 3
Designing Environmental Taxes

Within the broad heading of environmental tax instruments, a number of distinct types of measure may be identified:

- *Measured emission taxes.* This group of market-based instruments are those that involve tax payments directly related to metered or measured quantities of polluting effluent. A tax per unit of measured pollution output of this sort conforms most closely to the type of tax envisaged in the early discussion by Pigou (1920) of the correction of externalities.
- *Use of other taxes to approximate Pigouvian taxes.* Changes in the rates of indirect taxes (excise duties, sales taxes or value added taxes) may be used as an indirect alternative to the explicit taxation of measured emissions. Goods and services that are associated with environmental damage in production or consumption may be taxed more heavily (e.g. carbon taxes, and taxes on batteries and fertilisers), whilst goods that are believed to benefit the environment may be taxed less heavily than their substitutes (e.g. the reduced taxes on unleaded petrol).
- *Non-incentive taxes.* In many cases, environmental taxes have in practice been used principally for purposes of revenue-raising, rather than to provide incentives to reduce polluting emissions (OECD, 1989). Where environmental taxes have been employed in this way, it has generally been to raise earmarked revenues for particular public expenditures related to environmental protection — for example, to recover the costs of administering a system of environmental monitoring or regulation, or to pay for public or private expenditures on pollution-abatement measures.

Current interest in environmental taxes principally concerns incentive applications, rather than the choice of earmarked revenue sources for particular functions. There are good reasons for this. Earmarking, to the extent that it genuinely constrains the level and dynamics of particular spending functions, is liable to lead to inefficiency in budgeting and expenditures. There is, it should be clear, no reason to wish expenditures on particular items to be governed by the revenues raised by a particular tax or charge. Where, on the other hand, earmarking does not affect the overall allocation of resources to particular budget heads, it amounts to little more than a deceptive presentational 'gloss', masking the real motives and processes in public revenue-raising and budgetary allocation. For example, where the budget headings receiving earmarked revenues also receive additional revenues from general tax revenues, the earmarking no longer determines the level of spending on the functions concerned; changes at the margin in the allocation of general revenues can offset — and 'undo' — all of the effects of the earmarking. The remainder of this report will, for these reasons, pay little further attention to the non-incentive role of environmental taxes, and will concentrate on the design and use of environmental taxes as incentive mechanisms.

Both of the incentive forms of environmental tax identified above have a role to play in environmental policy — those where tax payments are *directly related* to polluting emissions and those where the environmental incentive is based on an *indirect* relationship between the amounts paid in tax and the environmental problem that the tax seeks to influence. The choice between a tax directly related to emission quantities and a tax that is more indirectly linked to the pollution it aims to control will depend on considerations of two sorts — administrative cost and 'linkage'. Often there will be a trade-off between lower administrative cost and better linkage. In many cases, environmental taxes based on measured emissions will have higher administrative costs than taxes that are levied on some other base, but will be better linked to the amount of pollution caused and will thus provide a more precisely-targeted incentive to reduce pollution. The balance between these two considerations is, however, likely to differ from case to case.

3.1 Administrative Cost

The administrative costs of any new tax will normally depend on how much scope there is for the tax to be incorporated in existing systems of administration and control. Where the assessment, collection or enforcement of the tax can be 'piggy-backed' on to corresponding operations already undertaken for existing taxes, the costs of an environmental tax measure may be significantly less than where wholly-new administrative apparatus and procedures are required.

The vast majority of existing taxes are levied on transactions — the value of goods and services sold, the value of incomes paid or received, etc. The scale economies that can be achieved from administrative integration of environmental taxes are likely to be greatest where environmental taxes, too, are levied in a form based on transaction values. Thus, for example, the differentiation of the rates of existing taxes (which may be seen as the limiting case of a tax reform closely compatible with existing tax administration) may gain considerably from combined administration. On the other hand, there are likely to be few gains from combining the administration of a tax on measured emission quantities with existing transaction-based taxes.

It is necessary to bear in mind that most administrative piggy-backing is unlikely to be wholly costless from the point of view of the administration of existing taxes. Greater complexity is likely to increase administrative costs in all areas — though the extent of this will depend on the existing degree of complexity in the tax structure.

New environmental taxes based on measured emissions quantities will require, as a minimum, the additional costs to be borne of a system for the assessment or measurement of the emission quantities on which the tax is to be levied. These costs will depend on the following:

- *Measurement costs per source.* These will vary depending on the technical characteristics of the emissions (flow, concentration, stability, etc.), the substances involved and the range of currently-available measurement technologies. Recent scientific and commercial developments in measurement and control are likely to have substantially widened the range of technologies available for monitoring the concentrations and flows of particular substances in effluent discharges, and hence to have increased the range of pollution problems for which charging on the basis of direct measurement is likely to be a feasible and cost-effective option. It is also probable that the *future* pace of development and commercialisation of such technologies will in part be stimulated by a greater use of direct emissions charging.
- *The number of emissions sources.* Direct charging for measured emissions quantities will be less likely to be worth while, the more separate emissions sources there are. An extreme case of this is non-point-source pollution — in other words, where no identifiable pipe, outlet or chimney provides a 'point source' at which emissions can be measured. The leaching of agricultural fertilisers and pesticides into the water system are examples of non-point-source pollution; for such pollution problems, direct measurement is likely to be costly and/or highly imprecise.
- *Scope for integration with normal commercial activities.* The costs of a system of emissions measurement

will generally be reduced if the measurement of emissions can be integrated with activities that would naturally take place for normal commercial reasons. Not merely does this reduce the additional costs of measurement for tax purposes, but it also tends to reduce the risk of false or misleading information being provided, since there are non-tax reasons for accurate measurement.

3.2 Linkage

Where the costs of an environmental tax system based on direct charging for measured emissions are high, restructuring of the existing tax system may provide an alternative way of introducing fiscal incentives to reduce environmental damage. The effectiveness of changes in the existing tax system in achieving an efficient pattern of pollution abatement will depend on the degree to which the taxation is closely linked to the pollution that it aims to control. If the tax rises, does it encourage taxpayers to seek to reduce this tax burden by reducing the processes or activities that give rise to polluting emissions, or are they, instead, just as likely to find ways to reduce their tax payments that do not change their level of pollution?

This issue of linkage is central to any case for or against using fiscal instruments other than those based on direct charging for measured emissions: where the linkage between tax base and pollution is weak, the tax may fail to have the desired impact on pollution, and may, at the same time, introduce unnecessary and costly distortions into production and consumption decisions.

'Indirect' environmental tax policies depend on the existence of a stable relationship between the tax base and pollution, but relationships that are observed to be stable in the absence of policy measures can turn out to be unstable once a tax is introduced. A good illustration of this phenomenon is given by Sandmo's (1976) account of

Norway's attempt to introduce a system of charging for domestic refuse collection by charging for the special sacks that householders were required to use for their refuse. The logic for the system was that the number of sacks used would be a rough proxy for the quantity of refuse collected from each household. Unfortunately, the charging scheme, once implemented, changed the relationship between sacks used and refuse collected. Some households tended to economise on sacks rather than to economise on refuse, and responded to the tax by overfilling the sacks or by dumping refuse, causing environmental problems elsewhere.

Where there is a wide range of available techniques which differ widely from one another in the relationship between tax base and pollution, linkage is likely to be more of a problem than where the range of technologies is small and the relationship between tax base and pollution is broadly stable across production techniques. Technical data about the range of available production techniques and their environmental attributes will thus help to assess the practical relevance of linkage problems for any particular environmental tax.

McKay, Pearson and Smith (1990) observe that a particularly severe problem of linkage arises where it is sought to influence pollution emissions from a production process through taxes on *inputs* and where significant scope exists for pollution abatement through effluent 'cleaning' at the end of the production process. One case in point is the scope for cleaning the sulphur dioxide emissions of coal-fired power-stations by fitting 'scrubbers' (flue gas desulphurisation equipment or FGDs). Where effluents can be cleaned in this way, taxes on production inputs will not be an effective way of encouraging an efficient pattern of pollution abatement. Such a tax (e.g. a tax on sulphurous coal) may discourage the use of polluting materials in production, but will provide no incentive to clean up effluents from the process. Although pollution may be reduced, the way in which pollution reductions are achieved will not necessarily be the most efficient.

Environmental taxes on fuel inputs may thus be more appropriate to deal with carbon dioxide emissions, where effluent cleaning is not currently a commercially-viable option, than in dealing with sulphur emissions, where important effluent-cleaning technologies are available.[5] However, it should be noted that what is at issue is not merely the existence of (commercially-viable) alternative technologies, but also the potential for them to be developed, since an efficient pollution tax will create an incentive for new technologies, involving less pollution, to be developed. The acceptability of a carbon tax on fuel inputs instead of a tax on measured carbon emission quantities depends in part on a judgement about how rapidly such technological developments are likely to take place, and about how far their future development might be inhibited by the choice of a tax on inputs rather than a tax on measured emissions.

---

[5] A number of countries, including Sweden and Finland, have already introduced carbon taxes on fuels (Hoeller and Wallin, 1991).

CHAPTER 4
Water

This chapter discusses the use of charges to address environmental problems of two distinct sorts relating to water. First, Section 4.1 considers the use of direct emissions charges on pollution discharged into the water system — into rivers, lakes, groundwater and, possibly, the sea. Here, the environmental objectives are relatively clear and unambiguous, and the role that could be played by incentive charges can be specified clearly. The use of emissions charges in Germany has been widely noted (see, for example, Royal Commission on Environmental Pollution (1992)); in the UK, charges are levied which have certain similarities, and which could form the basis for development of a more extensive incentive charging system.

Sections 4.2 and 4.3 then discuss a different set of environmental issues, those relating to water abstraction and water use. In general, the environmental effects of water abstraction are less straightforward, and the requirements for incentives to promote efficiency more complex, than in the case of water pollution. Section 4.2 discusses the role of direct abstraction charges; Section 4.3 then considers the impact of water pricing for supplies to households on the efficiency of water use and on environmental objectives.

4.1 Emissions Charges

Environmental taxes on water pollution

Water pollution is regulated in most European countries primarily through 'command-and-control' forms of regulation, which either set maximum permitted levels for emissions or require the use of particular pollution-control technologies. A number of countries operate systems of user charges for water emissions, as mechanisms for raising revenues for water pollution control, alongside the basic framework of command-and-control regulation. In at least three of the European systems with revenue-raising water charges — France, Germany and the Netherlands — there has been considerable analysis of the potential for these charge systems also to have some incentive effect (Bower, Barre, Kuhner and Russell, 1981; Bongaerts and Kraemer, 1989; Andersen, 1994).

Emissions charges in Germany

Water pollution charges in Germany were introduced from 1981 under the Federal Republic's 1976 Wastewater Charges Act (Abwasserabgabengesetz, AbwAG). The charges were introduced in 1981 in three states (Länder) — Schleswig-Holstein, Hessen and Saarland — and then extended, covering the whole Federal Republic from 1983. Following reunification, the system has been extended to former East Germany in two stages — enterprises already subject to an emissions charge under the legislation of former East Germany became subject to the federal Abwasserabgabe in 1991, and the system was fully extended to former East Germany with effect from the start of 1993.

The charges are levied on direct discharges into rivers, lakes, the sea and groundwater by both industrial and municipal sources. Indirect discharges, by sources discharging into the treatment systems of municipalities, are not charged.

The charging system is based on a formula, under which pollution units, broadly equivalent to the pollution generated by one individual, are defined for each of a range of pollutants, including chemical oxygen demand (COD), phosphorus, nitrogen, some organic compounds and some metals; one unit is, for example, equivalent to 50 kilograms of COD or 20 grams of mercury (Table 4.1).

TABLE 4.1

Weighting of different pollutants in German effluent charge

	Pollutant weight corresponding to one unit
Chemical oxygen demand	50kg of oxygen
Phosphorus	3kg
Nitrogen	25kg
AOX (adsorbable organic halogens)	2kg, calculated as organic bound chlorine
Mercury	20g
Cadmium	100g
Chromium	500g
Nickel	500g
Lead	500g
Copper	1kg

The charges were introduced gradually, starting in 1981 at a rate of DM12 (£2.63) per unit, and have then been increased in annual stages, to DM60 (£24.16) per unit in 1993. A further increase, to DM70 per unit, is scheduled for 1997 (Table 4.2).

The waste water charge law is closely related to the water management law (Wasserhaushaltsgesetz, WHG), also introduced in 1976. This defined permit and licence requirements for all abstractors and dischargers of water.

TABLE 4.2

Rates of German effluent charge

As from 1 January:	*DM per unit*
1981	12
1982	18
1983	24
1984	30
1985	36
1986	40
1991	50
1993	60
1997 (planned)	70

These requirements are, in general terms, that discharges should not exceed the generally-recognised technology rules, or best available technology (BAT) standards for hazardous substances.

A distinctive feature of the emissions charging system which is intended to reduce measurement costs is that charges are normally based on expected volume and concentration for the year ahead. These values (Überwachungswerte) correspond to the discharge permit limits agreed under the Wasserhaushaltsgesetz. Compliance is largely self-monitored, although subject to random spot checks. The frequency of spot checks varies depending on the size of the plant and the substances discharged.

Measurements that show non-compliance result in penalties reflecting the highest observed discharge level; a single discharge in excess of the agreed level results in an increase in charges equal to half the excess level of emissions, whilst more than one breach results in the full excess being charged (Sprenger, Körner, Paskuy and Wackerbauer, 1994, p. 102).

Charges can be reduced in certain circumstances, such as where state-of-the-art abatement technologies are used or where the polluter constructs or significantly improves a sewage treatment plant.

For chemical oxygen demand and suspended solids, reductions in charges are based on compliance with the generally-recognised technical rule (allgemein erkannte Regel der Technik) for abatement technology and practice. Dischargers meeting this standard are liable to only 50 per cent of the unit charge, whilst those reducing pollution to less than 50 per cent of this standard are exempt altogether from the charge.

Prior to 1989, similar rules for charge reductions applied to discharges of halons and heavy metals. Since 1989, however, operators meeting best available technology (Stand der Technik) standards with regard to discharges of halons and heavy metals are liable to only 20 per cent of the unit charge.

An operator can reduce the agreed level of charged emissions on the basis of a discharger's declaration (Erklärung des Einleiters) to the effect that a level of emissions will be maintained at least 20 per cent below the initial discharge level for at least the next three months; the charge due is then reduced by a corresponding percentage. Failure to respect the new levels gives rise to the same penalties for non-compliance as apply to higher discharge levels.

In order to avoid increasing the overall fiscal burden on direct dischargers, the system allows dischargers to offset the costs of investment in pollution-control equipment against charges. First, an operator planning to build a water treatment plant that will result in a cut of at least 20 per cent in emissions can benefit from a corresponding proportionate reduction in charges for the three years prior to building the new plant. Second, from 1987, a discharger building a treatment plant that will reduce emissions to under 50 per cent of the generally-recognised technical rule can offset half the cost of the investment against charges in the year of construction and the two subsequent years.

The charges are administered by the Länder, although the rates applied are uniform across the country. The revenues accrue to the Länder, which are required to use them for certain defined categories of expenditure, including waste water treatment facilities, and research and development in techniques for improving water quality. Aggregate revenues in 1990 were about DM340 million (£118 million). Costs of administration of some DM50 million (£17 million) accounted for a significant proportion of this, about 15 per cent of the gross revenue.

Sprenger et al. (1994) evaluate the performance of the Abwasserabgabengesetz (AbwAG) against the following criteria: ecological efficiency, economic efficiency, distributional effects, budgetary effects and administrative practicality; their analysis is extensive, and only some of the conclusions in relation to the first two criteria are summarised here. They observe that the information basis for evaluation is limited in some key respects; thus, for example, no systematic official investigation of the outcomes of the system has been undertaken, no data exist on the extent to which use has been made of the opportunities for reductions in the unit charge, on the pattern of revenues according to the particular pollutants, or on the sectoral pattern of source and use of the charge revenues. Also, they argue that there are significant conceptual difficulties in conducting an evaluation of the impact of the AbwAG alone, given that it is so closely bound up with the regulatory system, through the use of the regulatory limits determined under the Wasserhaushaltsgesetz (WHG) as the initial basis for charging. Thus, although it is unquestionable that the introduction of the charge has been associated with a significant reduction in emissions of the charged pollutants, it is not possible to attribute this immediately to the effect of the charge, since it could equally reflect the impact of the changes in regulatory limits under the WHG.

Evidence assessed by Sprenger et al. (1994) on the effectiveness of the charging system in reducing environmental damage related mainly to the early years of the policy, including the period before the charges came into force. Ewringmann, Kibat and Schafhausen (1980) questioned 92 enterprises and 46 municipalities during the 1974–79 'announcement phase' of the AbwAG, finding that three-quarters of the enterprises and two-thirds of the municipalities had increased, accelerated or modified their water pollution abatement measures under the combined pressure of the expected introduction of the measures in the AbwAG and the WHG. For two-fifths of the enterprises, this anticipatory response could be traced predominantly to the AbwAG. Sprenger and Pupeter

(1980), in another early investigation of the effects of the new legislation amongst 54 major industrial direct dischargers, observed an extensive acceleration of abatement measures; they argued that this appeared to be largely the result of the charge, since the increased investment appeared to be much the same for firms that were not required to change their behaviour by the regulatory system under the WHG as for those that were.

Further beneficial ecological effects observed by Sprenger et al. (1994) arise through the incentive that the charge gives for more careful management of abatement facilities, from possible beneficial ecological side-effects through the reduction of uncharged forms of emission, as a by-product of measures to reduce emissions of charged substances, and from various types of 'soft effect' in terms of changes in attitudes and awareness of companies, municipalities and their employees. Less desirable aspects of the system from an ecological perspective included the lack of a systematic ecological rationale for the relative levels of charge applied to different substances, and the lack of regional differentiation in the charge to reflect differences in the ecological vulnerability of different areas.

As regards economic efficiency, the conclusion of Sprenger et al. (1994) is that the system has some significant deficiencies, which restrict the extent to which it achieves the efficiency gains that would in principle be attainable from an economic instrument. First, the close relationship between the charging system and the system of regulatory permits does not allow the cost-minimising pattern of abatement to be chosen freely by polluters; instead, many of the abatement measures undertaken are dictated by the pattern required by permit conditions. Second, there is a potential for distortion in competition between direct and indirect dischargers, arising through the fact that only direct dischargers are subject to the charge system. Third, the use of the revenues may not induce much behavioural modification; there may be a substantial 'dead weight' (Mitnahmeeffekt) of payments to enterprises that would have undertaken the measures without subsidy. Fourth, the reduction in the charge applicable to enterprises that 'overcomply' with the permit requirements reduces the tax burden on residual units of pollution, thus weakening the dynamic incentive function of the charge. The result, they argue, is that the tax is only really paid by those who resist the official norms, and it has thus become, in effect, an enforcement mechanism for these norms (Sprenger et al., 1994, p. 132).

Emissions charges in the UK

Polluting emissions to the water system in the UK are regulated through a system of discharge 'consents', which specify for a particular operator the maximum levels of permitted emissions. The system is operated by the National Rivers Authority (NRA), which took over the regulatory and environmental functions previously performed by the water authorities, following privatisation of the water industry under the Water Act 1989.

A system of discharge consent charges is levied by the NRA. Charges for the consents are intended, in the long run, to raise revenues sufficient to cover the administrative costs of the NRA in administering, monitoring and enforcing the system of consents. This position will be reached gradually, as existing, uncharged, consents expire and are replaced with new consents.

Initially, from October 1990, the NRA introduced a standard one-off £350 charge for determining new or revised consents; this charge has been increased over time, and currently stands at £504.[6] Later, from April 1994,

---

[6] In certain circumstances, a reduced charge applies; initially, this was set at £50, and it is currently £72. The reduced charge applies where the discharge

charges were introduced to cover the recurring costs of monitoring effluents and controlled waters. This system of charges is based on the maximum permitted volume of effluent specified in the discharger's consent, and varies depending on the content and destination of the effluent. A uniform national tariff applies; there is no regional differentiation based, for example, on local differences in assimilative capacity. Illustrative calculations for some hypothetical dischargers reported by the Royal Commission on Environmental Pollution (1992, p. 158) suggest that the NRA's cost recovery charge might be between a half and a quarter of the level of the German charge (at the 1991 rate of DM50 per unit).

The structure of the tariff is intended to reflect the costs that each discharger imposes in terms of monitoring and compliance work, rather than the pollution damage of the effluent. Thus the tariff rises with the size of discharge, but less than proportionately with volume, since monitoring costs do not rise proportionately. Similarly, the weightings in the charge formula for chemical content and destination reflect monitoring cost rather than relative pollution damage, although since more-detailed monitoring will be appropriate for discharges of greater toxicity, there is a tendency for costs to be higher for more-damaging emissions than for less-damaging emissions.

Appraisal

It is clear that, whatever their origin and initial purpose, the charges or taxes levied on water pollution in both Britain and Germany have the potential to have incentive effects on polluters' decisions. However, in both countries, the current structure of the charges and taxes levied

---

is less than 5m^3 per day of sewage effluent, trade effluent from cooling under 10m^3 per day or surface water not containing trade effluent.

may not maximise the potential for environmental and economic gains from the use of economic instruments in water pollution control.

As far as charges for polluting emissions to water from measurable 'point sources' are concerned, Germany's charges, in principle, conform rather more closely in structure to the optimal pattern of relative incentives than those in the UK. Nevertheless, the UK charges, which have been implemented solely for the purposes of cost recovery, are not of a wholly-different order of magnitude when compared with the German system, and might be expected also to have incentive effects on emissions. The German charge system significantly reduces the breadth of its incentive effect and the tax burden on polluters through a range of provisions for reduction or offsetting of the charge. The UK charge, whilst at a lower basic level, is applied more uniformly.

Incremental modification of both systems could greatly increase their environmental impact. Raising the rate of charge would be one aspect of this; restructuring could also lead to a more-efficient structure of abatement incentives.

Neither country has yet exploited the scope for using economic instruments to regulate non-point sources of water pollution — especially pesticide and fertiliser use. Examples of taxes for this purpose exist in some EU countries (including Austria). Evidence on their effectiveness is, however, sparse, and it is clear that such taxes would provide a somewhat rough-and-ready incentive, with only limited scope for differentiation according to local environmental conditions. Despite this, there may be gains from using taxes to discourage excessive use of fertilisers and pesticides; given the impossibility of directly measuring the amounts used, regulatory policies face severe practical limitations, and may have to involve costly and onerous regulatory monitoring and interference.

4.2   Charges for Water Abstraction

Environmental arguments for reducing water abstraction

In Britain and in some states of Germany, there are systems of charges for water abstraction — in other words, for taking water from surface water or groundwater sources for use by industry or households. How far might these charging schemes be seen as 'green' incentive mechanisms, similar in philosophy and function to environmental taxes?

One reason for levying abstraction charges would be to discourage over-exploitation of a common property resource. The amount of water available is limited, and unrestricted abstraction by some users could reduce the amount or quality of water available for others. How far this is a problem will depend on the amount of water available; in countries where water is scarce, unregulated abstraction can impose severe externalities on other users. In both Britain and Germany, any significant adverse impact of unregulated abstraction on water availability is likely to be confined to certain areas.

TABLE 4.3

Water abstraction, 1990

		Billion m^3
	Germany	*UK*
Total	58.9	14.2
Surface water	51.1	11.5
Groundwater	7.7	2.7
Total per capita (m^3)	740	281

Source: Umweltbundesamt, *Daten zur Umwelt 1992/93*, p. 326.

Abstraction may also have effects on the environment, of a number of sorts:

- in coastal areas, excessive abstraction of groundwater can result in saline sea water penetrating an aquifer and ruining the value of the aquifer as a source of non-saline water;
- excessive surface water abstraction from lakes or rivers can reduce their assimilative capacity for 'processing' pollutants, by increasing pollutant concentrations;
- some uses of abstracted water, for example, for cooling power-stations, can have significant adverse environmental effects when the abstracted water is later returned; a system regulating water abstraction may help to regulate these environmental effects.

Whilst a number of environmental consequences of water abstraction can be identified, these do not seem to be very well suited to efficient regulation through market incentives. Many of the effects are largely confined to particular geographical locations, and general incentives, not differentiated by location, will be liable to lead to excessive incentives in some areas or inadequate incentives in other areas, or both.

TABLE 4.4

Water abstraction, by use, 1990

	m^3 per capita	
	Germany	*UK*
Public water supply	85	132
Irrigation	23	3
Industry (excluding cooling)	35	17
Electrical cooling	514	47
Other	83	82
Total	740	281

Source: OECD, *Environmental Data Compendium 1993*, p. 55.

Water abstraction charges in Germany

In the German state of Baden-Württemberg, a charge for
water abstraction from groundwater and surface water
sources (the Wasserpfennig) has been levied since 1987.
The charge is based on the volume of water abstracted,
although the rates of charge per cubic metre vary depending on the source and the use to which the water is put
(Table 4.5). Small abstractions of less than 2,000m³ per
annum are exempt from the charge, and abstractions between 2,000m³ and 3,000m³ pay 50 per cent of the rate.
Substantial rebates, of up to 90 per cent, apply to production processes that are particularly water-intensive.

The revenues from the abstraction charge have aver-
aged some DM150 million annually since 1988 (equivalent to some £60 million at 1993 exchange rates). There
is an informal relationship between the revenues from the
Wasserpfennig and a programme of expenditures ('Ecology Programme') that includes, amongst other things,
subsidies paid to reduce the use of chemical fertilisers and
pesticides in areas where groundwater or surface water is
used by households or industry. The original intention
when the Wasserpfennig was proposed was that it should
provide revenues to finance these subsidy arrangements,
but the idea of a formal link was abandoned when doubts
were raised as to whether it would have been constitu-

TABLE 4.5

**The Baden-Württemberg Wasserpfennig:
rates of charge for water abstraction, 1993**

	DM per m³	*Equivalent in pounds per 1,000m³*
Groundwater abstraction	0.10	40
Public water supply	0.10	40
Surface water for irrigation	0.01	4
Surface water for cooling	0.01	4
Surface water for other purposes	0.04	16

tional. Nevertheless, despite the absence of formal ear-marking of the revenues, the Ecology Programme receives revenues equal to the level of the receipts from the abstraction charge.

It is to be expected that levying a charge for water abstraction would have reduced the volumes of water abstracted; the fact that revenues have tended to decline may be a sign that this has indeed occurred. Whether, however, there is a significant environmental gain from reducing levels of water abstraction is less clear. Klepper (1992), for example, is sceptical, arguing that shortage of water is 'unlikely to constitute the dominating environmental problem in Baden-Württemberg'. It seems clear that the initial logic of the system was seen primarily as a means to raise revenues for subsidies to reduce certain forms of water pollution, rather than as an effective 'green' incentive in its own right.

Other German states also levy charges for water abstraction:

- Berlin levies a groundwater withdrawal fee at a rate of DM0.30 per m³.
- Hamburg levies a water withdrawal fee (known as a 'lending fee') similar to the Baden-Württemberg Wasserpfennig, although it is based on permitted, rather than actual, abstractions. The main rates are DM0.15 per m³ for groundwater and DM0.10 per m³ for public water supply.
- Hessen has levied a groundwater withdrawal charge at rates of DM0.10–0.50 per m³ since June 1992.
- In the new Länder, the former GDR's water use fee is being replaced by abstraction charges, generally similar to the Baden-Württemberg scheme.

Water abstraction charges in the UK

Since 1969, charges have been levied in the UK for water abstraction, initially by the river authorities (later, regional water authorities) and since the Water Act 1989, by the National Rivers Authority (NRA).

The charges are set at a level to cover the cost of providing and operating certain services, such as reservoirs to regulate water flow, in each region. The regional variations in the charge thus reflect this revenue-raising requirement, rather than any assessment of the pressure that different uses place on water availability or environmental problems associated with water abstraction. On the other hand, the other elements in the calculation reflect, to some extent, the pressure placed by different uses on water availability; costs are higher for summer abstractions than for winter ones, and for abstractions that do not eventually return much of the abstracted water to the system.

The charges are based on the annual licensed volume for which the user has a licence and on the area, the source of the water, the season and the use to which the abstracted water will be put. The total charge payable is given by multiplying the licensed volume by the relevant source,

TABLE 4.6

National Rivers Authority charges for water abstraction: multiplicative factors for source, season and 'loss', 1995–96

		Factor
Source factor	Unsupported	1.0
	Supported	3.0
	Tidal	0.2
Season factor	Summer	1.6
	Winter	0.16
	All year	1.0
Loss factor	High loss *(e.g. spray irrigation)*	1.0
	Medium loss *(e.g. public water supply, general agricultural and industrial purposes)*	0.6
	Low loss *(e.g. mineral washing)*	0.03
	Very low loss *(e.g. power-station cooling, fish farms)*	0.003

Note: Certain rivers are designated 'supported sources'; all other sources (except tidal sources) are defined as unsupported sources.

TABLE 4.7

National Rivers Authority charges for water abstraction, 1995–96

Region	Standard unit charge (£ per 1,000m³)
Anglian	13.94
Northumbria	16.22
North West	7.98
Severn Trent	8.44
Southern	10.28
South West	12.50
Thames	7.95
Welsh	7.76
Wessex	11.00
Yorkshire	6.29

season and loss factors (shown in Table 4.6) and by the standard charge per unit for the region in which the abstraction is made (Table 4.7). For example, the holder of a licence in the North West region for 100,000m³ per annum for general industrial purposes (i.e. 'medium loss') from a river all year round would pay a charge given by the calculation shown in Box 4.1. The equivalent Baden-Württemberg Wasserpfennig charge for this example would probably be about £1,600, more than three times the NRA charge; however, since the structure of the

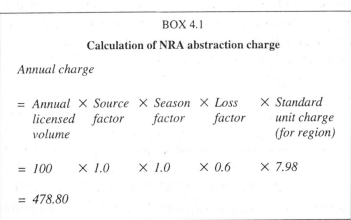

BOX 4.1

Calculation of NRA abstraction charge

Annual charge

= Annual × Source × Season × Loss × Standard
  licensed factor   factor   factor unit charge
  volume   (for region)

= 100 × 1.0 × 1.0 × 0.6 × 7.98

= 478.80

charges varies considerably between the two systems, the relative charge levels for other examples could be very different.

Appraisal

As with the charges for polluting emissions to the water system that were discussed in the previous section, it is clear that, in principle, the water abstraction charges levied in both the UK and Germany could have incentive effects, reducing the level and modifying the pattern of water abstraction. However, there may be rather less to be gained, from the point of view of environmental policy, from seeking to enhance the system of abstraction charges than from modification of existing emissions charges. Although excessive water use can lead to environmental problems (for example, by increasing the vulnerability of rivers or underground aquifers to pollution damage), the scale of these problems in either Britain or Germany taken as a whole seems likely to be small.

Nevertheless, in particular localities, water abstraction may have much greater environmental significance and requires some form of policy control. However, for this to be achieved through economic instruments would require considerable modification of the existing abstraction charges, and also further measures relating to water use charging, to ensure that the incentive signal was transmitted effectively to water consumers. An optimal incentive policy would, for example, need to be tailored to the areas where abstraction causes the most acute problems, and neither of the current systems of abstraction charges in the UK or Germany does this or is designed to do so. What would be required for abstraction charges to reflect the environmental costs of taking water from groundwater or surface water sources would be a structure of charges that differed widely between areas; little environmental supplement would be needed to the existing charge in many areas, but in some localities the environmental component would perhaps be substantial. This may raise doubts as to the environmental gains that would result from efforts to reorientate the UK charging system in this direction. In addition, however, extension of abstraction charges in this way would have only limited effectiveness if the higher charges were not directly fed through to water users, as an incentive for reduced water consumption.

4.3 Volumetric Charging for Domestic Water Use

Higher charges for water abstraction could thus be used to ensure that the environmental costs of water abstraction are reflected in the costs of water supply and use. Particularly-high charges for certain sources of water where environmental pressures are most acute might induce substitution to water sources with a less adverse environmental impact. However, this is only one way of reducing problems of excessive water use and abstraction. In addition, charging mechanisms may be used to restrict the level of water *demand*, thus reducing the extent to which it is necessary to make use of water drawn from the most environmentally vulnerable sources.

Where abstractors themselves are the water consumers, higher abstraction charges would have a direct effect of this sort on water use. However, where water is not abstracted by the end-user, but by an intermediary supplier of water to end-users, higher costs of abstraction will only lead to reduced water use if the charges for water supply levied by the intermediary reflect the actual quantities of water used. For efficient water consumption decisions, payments for water use must be related directly to the actual quantities of water used, and the price per unit should reflect the full private and social marginal costs of supply.

In both Britain and Germany, industrial users of water are, in the main, charged according to the quantity of water they use (although some smaller non-household consumers in the UK pay on a basis that does not directly reflect measured use). For household consumers, however, there is a sharp contrast between Germany, where volumetric charging for household water supply and sewerage services is the rule, and Britain, where charges for the overwhelming majority of households do not vary according to the amount of water they use. Thus, while in Germany the water charging system can transmit the environmental costs of water supply to household consumers as a well-linked incentive signal for water conservation, household water use in the UK takes place at a marginal cost of zero, and there is no incentive for consumers to modify their behaviour to take account of the costs of water supply.

Given the relatively limited environmental pressures that, as has been argued above, appear likely to be caused by water abstraction in both Britain and Germany, there is certainly room for argument about the extent to which an extension of volumetric charging for household water consumption in the UK is an environmental policy issue of any significance. The main value from an extension of consumption-related water charging would, instead, be efficiency gains, if reductions in water consumption proved a cheaper way of balancing water supply and demand than new, costly, water supply infrastructure investments. If reductions in water demand mean that one less additional reservoir must be built, the main gains from this are probably more the saving of unnecessary investment expenditures than the environmental benefits.

Nevertheless, there are reasons to consider water charges in this discussion of environmental tax and charge measures. One is that the water charge case illustrates more general issues concerning linkage and the efficient targeting of incentives. Another is that the charging arrangements for water supply and sewerage services are closely linked in both countries, and important issues arise about distribution of the burden of paying for the various environmental improvements in the water and sewerage field, particularly sewage treatment, that are financed by the charges levied on households for water consumption.

Charges for water and sewerage services in Germany

In Germany, water supply and sewerage services are, generally, supplied by different undertakings: water is generally supplied on a commercial basis by water supply companies (although many of these are under municipal ownership), whilst sewerage services are provided directly as a municipal service and financed within the municipal budgets.

Water supply tariffs and prices are set by the water supply companies, subject to the provisions of the general legislation against monopoly abuse. Water is generally charged for according to metered consumption, with consumers paying a two-part charge consisting of a relatively small standing charge and a volumetric charge per cubic metre consumed. In general, the volumetric charge accounts for some 90 per cent of the total bill. There is considerable variation between areas in the charge per cubic metre; the average in 1993 was some DM3.00 per cubic metre, with a range from a minimum of about DM1.50 in the areas with the lowest charges up to nearly DM5.00 per cubic metre in the most expensive areas (Kraemer, 1994, pp. 103–4). On the basis of a 'typical' household consumption of 96 cubic metres per annum, this would imply an annual household water bill in an area with average water prices of some DM320 (£143).

Herrington (1994) observes that, in contrast to the UK, where household water demand has been growing steadily in recent years (by some 16 per cent over the period 1980–91), household water demand in Germany appears to have been broadly static for some time. The per capita level of household water consumption in Germany could, according to Herrington's figures, be some 8 to 12 per cent lower than that in England and Wales. He notes two possible explanations for the difference — one is that the level (and rate of increase) of water prices and the extensive use of volumetric charging in Germany have restrained water demand, and the other is that the greater 'green consciousness' in Germany has affected both household use of water and the design of water-using appliances.

Sewerage services are generally also charged according to water consumption; the average rate per cubic metre was some DM2.70 in 1993. In addition, the practice is growing in many municipalities of also collecting a fee for rainwater drainage services computed on a separate basis, generally based on the size of the land area covered by buildings, tarmac and other impermeable ('sealed') surfaces.

Charging for sewerage services is constrained by a series of legal principles which, amongst other things, require charges to reflect the benefit a user derives from the service and also the specific costs of supply, and which require each user to be treated in the same way. These general legal requirements, however, interact both with political concerns to ensure that the charges levied are socially acceptable and with the practical difficulties of direct measurement of the services actually supplied. In comparison with water supply, where the service supplied can be directly measured by the volume of water supplied, using water use as a proxy for the use of sewerage services clearly reflects the choice of a pragmatic approximation to the level of service. However, the legal requirement that where differences in services supplied can be identified, these should be reflected in the charges levied has been the driving force behind the development of separate charges for collecting and treating rainwater run-off, based on a closer proxy to the likely costs of rainwater services associated with each property (Kraemer and Piotrowski, 1995).

Separating water and sewerage charges in this way, so
that certain sewerage services are no longer wholly
charged according to the volume of water consumed, is
liable to improve the efficiency of water consumption
decisions. Even where water consumption is a good proxy
for consumption of sewerage services, levying charges for
sewerage services based on the volume of water used
would be liable to result in inefficiently-low levels of
water consumption,[7] since it could increase the cost of
each cubic metre of water above the marginal cost of *water
supply*. As Kraemer and Piotrowski (1995) observe, dis-
sociating the charges for general sewerage services from
the charge for rainwater services could therefore increase
water demand. However, they also note that some municipalities offer reductions in the rainwater run-off charge to
households that use rainwater for watering, washing or
other purposes, so avoiding direct and immediate disposal,
and argue that the consequent reductions in demand for
piped water supplies could conceivably cancel out any
increase in water demand due to the reduced unit price.

Charges for water and sewerage services in the UK

Since privatisation of the former public-sector water
authorities in December 1989, water and sewerage services in the UK have been provided by the private sector.
About three-quarters of households in England and Wales
receive water and sewerage services from the 10 water
supply and sewerage companies privatised in 1989, whilst
the remainder receive water supplies from some 20
smaller water companies, and sewerage services from one
of the 10 major water supply and sewerage companies.

---

[7] From the point of view of sewerage services, too, reducing water use could
in certain circumstances increase the costs of sewerage services — for
example, by reducing rates of flow or increasing concentration.

The average household bill for water and sewerage services in 1995–96 is £211 in England and Wales (OFWAT, 1995); of this, the water component accounts for slightly less than half (47 per cent on average, or some £99).[8] Household bills vary widely between companies — for the water supply component in 1995–96, the highest average bill was £158 (South East Water) and the lowest £72 (Portsmouth).

The majority of businesses pay water charges based on consumption; only some 24 per cent of non-household customers were charged on an unmeasured tariff in 1995–96. Business measured charges reflect volumes, and also the supply pipe size, which may be seen as an indicator of peak demand.

The majority of households pay bills based on the unmeasured tariff. However, since privatisation, the number of households with a metered water supply has been rising steadily, from about 330,000 households in England and Wales in 1990–91 to about 1.4 million (7 per cent of all households) in 1995–96. The proportion of households metered varies between companies, from less than 1 per cent for Northumbrian Water and for some of the smaller companies, to 17 per cent of customers of Anglian Water and South East Water (OFWAT, 1995, p. 39). The rise in metering has taken place for two main reasons. One is that meters have generally been installed in new houses, for which rateable values do not exist. The other reason for greater take-up of metering is that, under pressure from the water regulator, OFWAT, there have been substantial reductions in the tariffs for measured supplies; in particular, most companies have made large reductions in the

---

[8] Average household water bills in England and Wales thus appear about one-third lower than the £143 calculated above for the 'typical' German household.

standing charge for measured supplies. Reflecting this, average measured bills fell in real terms by 3.2 per cent between 1989–90 and 1994–95, whilst unmeasured bills rose by one-third in real terms over the same period (CRI, 1994).

What would be the consequences of moving to a more widespread use of volumetric charging in the UK, with domestic water charges based on metered water consumption rather than on rateable value or other quasi-tax bases? Amongst the range of costs and benefits that would need to be taken into account, distributional impacts have had considerable prominence in the public debate, and the scope for efficiency gains would need to be balanced against the social and political consequences of a considerable redistribution of the current burden of water charges. A number of observations may be made, about both distributional and efficiency effects of volumetric charging.

First, as regards the distributional impact, research by Rajah and Smith (1993) using data from the UK Family Expenditure Survey, supplemented by water-use data

FIGURE 4.1

Metered charges for domestic water supplies and charges based on domestic property values, as a percentage of income

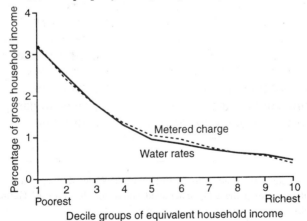

Source: Rajah and Smith, 1993, Figure 4.

from a water company survey, suggests that charges based on water metering would, in fact, have a very similar distributional incidence across income groups to the incidence of the existing charges (Figure 4.1). The average proportion of household income taken in metered charges would be almost the same amongst the poorest income groups, would be slightly higher than with water rates for middle income groups, and slightly lower for the richest income group. The scale of the redistribution in relation to household income does not appear to be a significant issue for policy.

However, considerably greater distributional effects would arise across household types as a result of the introduction of universal water metering (Figure 4.2). Large households would tend to lose, whereas smaller

FIGURE 4.2

Gains and losses from a switch from property tax finance of domestic water supplies to metered charging

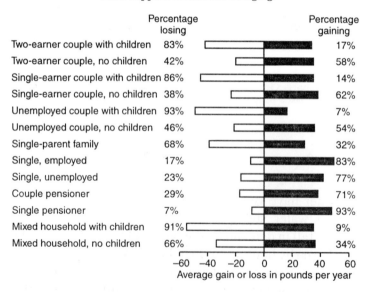

Note: Mixed households are all households that do not fall into the other categories shown, and include mixed pensioner and non-pensioner households and households with more than two adults.

Source: Rajah and Smith, 1993, Figure 5.

48

households would tend to gain. The highest proportion of losers can be found amongst households consisting of unemployed couples with children, whereas 93 per cent of single-pensioner households gain. This pattern of gainers and losers reflects the strong correlation between household size and water consumption.

Second, concerning the efficiency effects of volumetric water charging, the potential savings in water supply costs (including environmental costs of water abstraction, new reservoir construction, etc.) would need to be balanced against the greater cost of operating the charging system. As discussed in Chapter 3, charges based on direct measurement involve dead-weight costs of the measurement system, which may be avoided where existing, or simpler, proxy bases are employed. The likely additional costs of metering are difficult to assess from current metering installation and reading costs, since there are probably considerable scale economies from co-ordinated installation and high-volume production and fitting. Some indication, however, is provided by the National Metering Trials project, in which metering experiments were undertaken in a number of trial areas. The final report of the project (Water Services Association et al., 1993) found that meter installation cost an average of £165 per property for an internal meter and £200 for an external meter. These costs, and any additional continuing costs of meter reading and information processing, need to be set against the net gains from more economical use of water by households. The latter have two components — first, the benefit of reduced water supply costs, resulting from the price-induced fall in demand, and, second, the welfare and other costs borne by households in reducing water consumption. Whilst the National Metering Trials report does not provide a comprehensive assessment of this sort, it does suggest that metering would be liable to lead to appreciable changes in water consumption levels, with at least scope for some savings in long-term supply costs. The

TABLE 4.8

The incentive for household take-up of metering, under four non-measured charging systems, based on the excess of non-measured charges over metered charge

Percentages of all households

	Households facing fiscal disincentive to choose metering		Households broadly indifferent to metering	Households facing fiscal incentive to choose metering	
Annual saving from metered charge:	*−£50 or more*	*−£25 to −£50*	*−£25 to +£25*	*+£25 to +£50*	*+£50 or more*
Flat-rate licence fee	16%	15%	17%	20%	32%
Charge based on number of household members	1%	11%	48%	28%	13%
Charge based on house type	13%	17%	18%	21%	31%
Charge based on property capital value	13%	18%	16%	24%	30%

Note: Due to rounding, rows do not necessarily add to 100.
Source: Rajah and Smith, 1993, Table 4.

average reduction in water consumption amongst the households in the trials was 11 per cent compared with supply on the unmetered tariff.

Third, as Rajah and Smith (1993) discuss, distributional and efficiency issues are linked, if (as is currently the situation in the UK) households are given the option of choosing between metered and non-metered charges. The economic gains from metering arise if metering induces households to reduce water use, where the value to them of some water uses is less than the charge levied for the water. Where water use is reduced by metering, the savings in water supply costs need to be balanced against the additional costs of meter installation and metering. Installing meters that do not result in a reduction in water use involves a simple dead-weight loss to the economy, in that the costs of metering are incurred without any saving in supply costs. In a system where households can choose whether to be metered or to pay a non-metered charge, there is a risk that households may choose to install meters without making any change in their water consumption, or that households that might reduce their consumption if metered do not take up the option of metering. This inefficiency arises if the distributional incidence of the two systems of charging differs too widely; then, most of the advantages or disadvantages that households would perceive from metering arise because of the difference between the two charging systems. Table 4.8 presents some estimates of the extent to which UK households might be encouraged to take up metering because they could save money without changing their behaviour, or be discouraged from taking up metering because it would cost them more, under four possible non-metered charging systems.

Fourth, recent German developments raise the question of whether it is appropriate to charge for sewerage services on the same basis as water supply, if water supply is charged according to volumes consumed. The development of separate rainwater run-off charges in Germany based on 'sealed' area rather than water consumption reflects the fact that water consumption can be a poor proxy for some aspects of sewerage services. Likewise, some of the components of water demand that would be expected to be most sensitive to volumetric charging (such as watering gardens) are likely to involve little corresponding reduction in the use made of sewerage services. In addition, it is possible to think of circumstances in which reductions in water use could increase rather than reduce the costs of sewerage services. This would suggest that, whether or not greater use is made of volumetric charging for domestic water supply in the UK, sewerage services should not also be charged according to the volume of water consumed.

CHAPTER 5
Waste

Public concerns about the environment and the environmental 'sustainability' of current patterns of production and consumption have been focused, above all, on the generation and disposal of waste. It is in this area where individual and community initiatives have been most prominent. Many households and local authorities in both Britain and Germany participate in recycling, and there is growing consumer resistance — perhaps more marked in Germany than in the UK — to excessive product packaging.

Public concern about the 'throw-away society' has had a number of aspects. One prominent anxiety has been that society is using up the earth's finite, non-renewable, resources of raw materials at an excessive rate, so that 'not enough' will be left for future generations.[9] This concern raises questions of resource-use policy which are important but beyond the environmental-policy focus of this report. There are, however, important environmental problems associated with waste generation and management which require attention. Moreover, there is, in this field, considerable scope for taxes and other incentive mechanisms to be employed as part of an efficient policy package.

---

[9] What would constitute an adequate legacy to future generations is addressed in Pearce, Markandya and Barbier (1989). A strong form of sustainability, in which the current generation leaves future generations with an unchanged stock of natural resources (natural capital), seems both unrealistic and an unnecessarily-restrictive requirement. A weaker requirement would be that future generations should receive at least as much total capital (aggregating natural resources and physical and intellectual capital) as the present generation inherited.

TABLE 5.1

Disposal of municipal waste

	Germany, 1990		UK, 1989	
			Million tonnes	
Incineration	4,742	(17%)	2,500	(13%)
Landfill	21,581	(77%)	14,000	(70%)
Other	1,635	(6%)	3,500	(18%)
Total	27,958		20,000	

Note: UK figures refer to household waste only.
Source: OECD *Environmental Data Compendium 1993*, p. 141.

The environmental issues concerning waste largely have to do with the environmental consequences of different methods of waste disposal — the pollution and amenity costs of landfill disposal, incineration, sea dumping, etc. Other forms of waste management besides disposal may also involve pollution and amenity costs. Glass recycling, for example, uses energy, and bottle banks and other collection methods could impose amenity costs — for example, of noise — on some local residents.

The generation of waste involves a series of decision-makers and interrelated decisions. Product manufacturers decide how products should be packaged. Consumers decide which products to purchase and whether to dispose of bottles, cans and other packaging in their household garbage or through a recycling facility. The public authorities or private firms that collect household waste decide what disposal option to employ — landfill, incineration or, where feasible, separation and recycling. The environmental problems of waste management arise because at each of these stages the decision-makers concerned do not face costs that reflect the full social costs of the choices that they make. In some cases, of course, decision-makers face no costs at all — households, for example, face a zero cost for waste disposal in the UK. In other cases, whilst decision-makers may face some costs such as, for example, the charges that public authorities may have to pay to the operators of landfill sites or incinerators, these costs do not reflect the social and environmental costs of choosing a particular course of action. In short, therefore, price signals may be wrong or non-existent.

There is clearly scope for using taxes on the various elements of the waste process to correct these faulty price signals, so that decision-makers at each stage of the process would face the full social costs of their actions. An efficient structure of prices would require, first, that appropriate charges or taxes were levied where environmental externalities or other social costs arise, and, second, that each stage in the waste 'chain' from product manufacturer to waste disposal were linked by an appropriate financial transaction.

Thus, to reflect air pollution externalities arising from waste incineration, for example, a tax might be levied on incinerator operators in proportion to the air pollution they cause; if this were reflected in the charges paid by local authorities for each tonne of waste sent to the incinerator, it would ensure that these environmental costs were taken into account in their choice of disposal option. Where all disposal options have environmental costs, it would be desirable for minimisation of waste to accompany switching of disposal option. However, for households and product manufacturers to face appropriate incentives for waste minimisation, charges must be levied on households that reflect the full costs of disposal of their household refuse; in this way, higher disposal costs can feed back into incentives for waste minimisation, through, for example, reduced packaging where this is the best option, taking all relevant social and private costs into account.

The difficulty for policy, however, is that it is unlikely to be practicable to levy appropriate taxes on all disposal options, or to ensure that the financial incentives link all of the relevant decision-makers. Illegal disposal (such as fly-tipping) remains, by definition, uncharged, and raising the costs of legal disposal options may encourage greater use of illegal routes, which could have costs in terms of disamenity or environmental damage. Transmitting the financial signals back may be difficult, too. Even where charges for the collection of household refuse seek to provide households with an incentive to minimise waste volumes, they rarely distinguish between different categories of waste according to their costs of disposal. Also, if increased household waste disposal costs are to provide an incentive for manufacturers to change the design of products and packaging, this depends not only on the *existence* of shifts in consumer demand towards products with lower disposal costs, but also on the ability of firms to *identify* correctly the shifts in demand and their reason.

5.1 Landfill Taxes

Landfill sites for waste disposal are becoming increasingly scarce, as existing sites are exhausted and as planning obstacles limit the development of new sites. This trend is becoming apparent in most industrialised countries and is forcing many to reappraise waste management strategies, to reduce reliance on landfill disposal and to increase the proportions of waste reused and recovered.

Where waste management is operated by decentralised agencies of government and by private-sector firms paying the full market rate for the landfill facilities they use, there is no obvious need for central government intervention to discourage the use of landfill disposal on grounds of future scarcity. Scarcity of landfill sites will be reflected in higher charges levied for their use by owners and operators, reflecting the opportunity cost of current landfill use in terms of the loss of future landfill capacity. In areas where landfill is becoming scarce, market forces should ensure that disposal of waste to landfill is correspondingly expensive.

Government intervention in waste management is, however, needed to regulate the externalities from landfill and other waste disposal options which are not reflected in the charges levied by operators. There are three principal externalities that may be relevant:

- current environmental externalities from landfill sites and other disposal options, including disamenity costs to local residents, polluting emissions in the form of greenhouse gases and 'conventional' air pollutants, damage through leaching into water systems, environmental costs of transporting waste to sites, etc.;
- future social costs which may arise if landfill operators make inadequate provision for the long-run costs of managing landfill sites and are able to avoid liability for these costs through bankruptcy or other means;
- possible social benefits from the alternatives to landfill; for example, if disposal through incineration leads to energy production which can substitute for more-polluting forms of energy supply.

A government-sponsored study of externalities from landfill and incineration in the UK (Department of the Environment, 1993) estimated two components of the externalities associated with landfill sites, one a 'fixed' element, not directly related to amounts disposed, reflecting the disamenity of the site to local residents, and the second a volume-related component. On the basis of studies for the US, it was suggested that the fixed 'disamenity' externality could be of the order of some £160 per household per year for households within four miles of the site, with negligible disamenity at greater distances from the site. The variable component of the externality from landfill sites would be about £3.4–4.1 per tonne of waste deposited in sites without provisions for energy recovery, and £1–2 per tonne in sites with energy recovery; methane emissions were estimated to account for a large part of these costs. On the other hand, waste incineration yielded social *benefits* of some £4 per tonne, once the benefits of energy recovery in the form of displacement of other air pollution are included. As a result, there would be a social difference between landfill and incineration of some £5–8 per tonne.

In Britain, the Chancellor of the Exchequer's Budget in November 1994 announced that the government intended to introduce a new tax on waste disposed in landfill sites. Further details of the proposed system were set out in a consultation paper (HM Customs and Excise et al., 1995) published in March 1995, which sought the views of industry and others about the proposals. The Chancellor's statement indicated that the government was considering a significant incentive charge raising 'several hundred million pounds'. The additional tax burden that this would impose on business would be offset by a corresponding reduction in the level of employer National Insurance contributions to be made when the tax entered into force; thus, the burden of taxation on business would remain constant, but the base of the tax would switch away from labour costs to waste disposal.

The consultation paper set out proposals for how the tax would be assessed and administered. The paper proposed that the tax should be an *ad valorem* tax on the charges levied by landfill site operators; it would be assessed and collected by HM Customs and Excise and, as far as possible, would be integrated with the mechanisms and procedures used for VAT, so as to minimise the additional administrative and compliance cost burdens. Whilst a particular rate for the tax was not proposed, the consultation paper estimated revenues for two rates, 50 per cent and 30 per cent. At a rate of 50 per cent, the tax would be likely to raise some £500 million annually, permitting a reduction in employer National Insurance contribution rates from the current main rate of 10.2 per cent to 10.0 per cent.

Strong criticisms were, however, made of the proposal to operate the tax as an *ad valorem* tax on the charges made by landfill operators. The key objection was that an *ad valorem* tax would be a poor proxy for the social costs that the tax should aim to reflect. The initial proposal had suggested that an *ad valorem* charge would tend to be higher for waste requiring more expensive landfill facilities, and therefore for the more damaging types of landfill waste, but, in addition, the *ad valorem* charge would also penalise facilities that operated to higher and more costly environmental standards. As a result of these objections, the basis of the landfill levy has been revised, and the levy is now to be based on the weight of landfilled waste. However, is weight any better than the site disposal fee as a proxy for the social costs of landfilling waste? Different categories of waste may have different environmental implications, and there would appear to be a strong case, if a charge based on waste is to be employed, for levying different rates of charge per tonne on different categories of landfilled waste. In particular, rubble and other inert construction wastes pose relatively few environmental problems when landfilled, and the appropriate charge per tonne would be much lower than for other types of waste.

In parallel with the landfill levy, the consultation paper made a proposal for 'environmental trusts', which could be financed primarily from rebates from the landfill tax. The trusts would be non-profit-making private-sector bodies engaged in the restoration of landfill sites or research into waste management; they would be required to provide services of general public value, and would not be permitted to provide services of direct benefit to their contributors. Rebates against the landfill levy would be available to landfill operators who made payments to the trusts. In effect, the landfill operators could choose whether to pay the landfill levy to government or to an environmental trust, except that the rebate against the landfill levy allowed for contributions to the environmental trusts would be limited to 90 per cent of their value, to ensure that contributors had an incentive to ensure that resources provided to the trusts were spent efficiently.

In Germany, too, a similar measure for charging waste disposal has been under discussion. The proposed waste charge (Abfallabgabe) is intended to raise the cost of disposal to reflect both the scarcity value of disposal space[10] and the present and future environmental externalities involved in landfill disposal. The scale of proposed charges, in terms of DM per tonne of various categories of waste, is set out in Table 5.2. The charges comprise two elements — an abatement charge, to reflect present and future environmental costs from landfill disposal, and a disposal charge, to reflect the opportunity cost of using up scarce landfill capacity. Whilst the highest charges, for hazardous waste requiring supervision, would reach DM200 per tonne, most waste would be charged at between DM25 and DM75 per tonne. Revenues, accord-

TABLE 5.2

Rates of the proposed German waste charge (Abfallabgabe)

			DM per tonne
Category		*Abatement charge (Vermeidungsabgabe)*	*Disposal charge (Deponieabgabe)*
A.	Hazardous waste requiring supervision	100	75–100
B.	Industrial and bulk waste	25	50
C.	Hardcore and excavated material	—	15
D.	Other waste	—	25

Note: Highest rate of disposal charge for category A waste applies to underground disposal and to highly-toxic material.
Source: Umweltbundesamt.

---

[10] Under current rules governing the pricing of publicly-operated facilities, charges can be levied to cover direct costs only, and scarcity rents of landfill sites may not, therefore, be reflected in the charges currently levied.

ing to Michaelis (1993), could be of the order of DM2.0–5.3 billion (equivalent to £0.9–2.4 billion).

Charge rates and revenues in the German Abfallabgabe proposal appear substantially higher than in the proposed UK landfill levy, although direct comparison of the German scale of charges per tonne and the *ad valorem* rates proposed for the UK is not straightforward. However, taking an 'average' disposal cost in the UK of some £10 per tonne, the landfill levy would amount to £5 per tonne at the 50 per cent rate, considerably lower than the £10–30 that the German system would charge for non-hazardous industrial and domestic waste. One important reason for the higher German rates is the intention that the Abfallabgabe should not only charge for environmental costs, but should also place a price on the future scarcity of landfill sites, to offset the existing omission of this element from the charges levied by landfill operators.[11] This is, in principle, an important difference in the context and objectives of the UK and German systems; the 'scarcity rent' argument for the German charge reflects the specific institutional rules and relationships in Germany, which prevent appropriate charges being levied to cover landfill scarcity. How far the scarcity rent of landfill sites is actually reflected in existing landfill pricing within the UK system is unclear. However, privatisation and contracting-out have led to more 'arm's length' relationships between the various parties involved in waste disposal in the UK, and have therefore increased the likelihood that all elements of the private costs of landfill use, including the opportu-

---

[11] Even so, the pricing of landfill scarcity may still be too low, even when the Abfallabgabe is in operation; Faber, Stephan and Michaelis (1988) estimated that in the mid-1980s, the uncharged opportunity cost of landfill disposal space in the state of Baden-Württemberg was of the order of DM260 per tonne, well above the Abfallabgabe rates.

nity costs of using up scarce landfill, will be appropriately charged.

The systems raise similar issues concerning their likely efficiency and effectiveness in operation:

- Both would encourage substitution away from landfill, although the extent of the likely substitution away from landfill towards disposal options such as incineration is difficult to predict in advance of experience.
- In both cases, less desirable substitution may also occur; the higher cost of landfill increases the gains to be made from illegal disposal, including unlicensed landfilling, and export of hazardous waste.
- Both systems would impose substantial additional costs, in the form of tax payments, on industrial sectors that make heavy use of landfill disposal, although in both cases the revenues raised provide scope for offsetting tax reductions (explicitly tied to the new tax in the case of the UK landfill levy) which could leave the overall burden of taxation on industry unchanged.
- Finally, in both cases, whilst the charges would encourage substitution in disposal, they would not provide any greater incentive for other behavioural changes, such as waste reduction through changes in product design and packaging, or greater household participation in waste separation and recycling, which would be important parallel elements in an efficient overall approach to waste management.

The sections below consider the use of fiscal or quasi-fiscal measures in both Britain and Germany which aim to act on other components of the overall 'chain' of waste generation and disposal.

5.2 Household Waste Charges

Both in Britain and Germany, arrangements for the collection and disposal of household waste currently provide households with little or no individual financial incentive to change the amount of waste requiring disposal.

In Britain, household refuse collection and disposal are provided free of charge by local authorities, although since the introduction of compulsory competitive tendering for this service, a high proportion of household refuse collection and disposal services are supplied by private-sector firms, under contract to the local authority to provide a defined standard of service. Whilst the cost of household waste disposal will affect the level of council tax that has to be levied, there is no direct link between waste disposal costs and the incentive for individual householders to reduce the amount of waste that requires disposal. If disposal costs for each tonne of household refuse rise, for example when existing cheap landfills are used up or through the imposition of the landfill levy, this will be transmitted to households through higher council tax. With higher costs for disposal, it may be desirable for households to reduce the amount of waste requiring disposal, but with a tax-financed service, there is no incentive for them to do so.

In Germany, rather than financing the service through general local taxation, explicit charges are levied for household waste collection and disposal. Here, too, however, the majority of municipalities levy charges for household waste collection and disposal on a basis which provides, at best, a very weak incentive to reduce the amount of household waste. Households typically pay for the collection of a bin of given size; in some areas, charges also vary depending on the frequency with which the household chooses to have the bin emptied. Whilst larger bins attract higher charges, the difference in charge rates is often relatively small, and the choice of size is often made on the basis of convenience, to meet the household's 'peak' demand, rather than to reflect its average level of waste disposal. It is therefore unlikely that the availability of different charges for different-sized bins provides much practical incentive for households to reduce the amount of household waste produced.

A number of German communities are, however, now experimenting with waste charges that reflect the amounts of waste generated, charging according to the volume or weight of waste collected from each household. Initiatives to experiment with volumetric or weight-based charging systems have been taken by a number of the federal states: in Nordrhein-Westfalen, Baden-Württemberg, Rhineland-Pfalz and Saarland, extensive trials covering a number of municipalities have been conducted of various systems for consumption-dependent waste charges. In addition, a number of individual communities have introduced new waste charging systems, independently of the experiments being co-ordinated by the states.

Amongst the systems that have been tried are

- weighing of individual containers;
- automated container identification, allowing records to be kept of which containers have been emptied, and hence charges to be levied based on number of containers, type and/or volume;
- revenue stickers, where households purchase stickers that have to be attached to bags or containers each time they are emptied.

The trials are intended to provide evidence on the technical feasibility and costs of different systems, and on the gains that may be made from volumetric or weight-based charging in terms of reductions in household waste, and hence in the social costs of disposal.

Evidence from the US, where a number of communities have for some years conducted well-documented schemes of volumetric or weight-based charging for domestic refuse, indicates that considerable reductions can be achieved in amounts of household waste, and hence in disposal costs (Repetto, Dower, Jenkins and Geoghegan,

1992). Against these, however, must be balanced the higher administrative costs of consumption-dependent charging of individual households as compared with tax finance, and (as with landfill taxation) the danger of stimulating undesirable disposal practices (householders wishing to avoid the charge may, for example, simply dump waste in the countryside). In practice, a key determinant of the success of the US systems in reducing waste has been whether the introduction of use-related charges was accompanied by measures to provide households with viable options to simple disposal, such as an expansion of kerbside recycling facilities. Without such parallel initiatives, the opportunities for households to reduce waste through legitimate means were limited, and the benefits that might offset the higher costs of levying the charges correspondingly small.

5.3 Packaging Taxes

If the environmental externalities in waste management are principally those of different disposal options, such as, for example, the disamenity to local residents from landfill sites and the emissions of various atmospheric pollutants from landfill and incineration, then it may be possible, in theory, to establish efficient incentives to control these environmental costs by a combined use of the two measures discussed above, namely:

- introducing environmental taxes, such as the proposed UK landfill levy, on different disposal options, to reflect the environmental costs they entail; and
- replacing municipal taxes for household waste collection and disposal which do not reflect the amounts of waste collected from each household by charges that are an accurate reflection of the waste collection and disposal costs that result from the individual household's behaviour.

Through these two measures, the costs of waste disposal are increased to reflect the environmental costs of each disposal option, and these increased costs are transmitted back to households through charges for household waste collection that reflect the quantities collected. Thus, the higher costs for disposal would be transmitted back as an incentive to households to minimise the amount of waste they generate.

In principle, it might then be possible to see further transmission of this incentive back to manufacturers and retailers, to manufacture and package products in such a way as to minimise the subsequent waste disposal costs that households will bear. Consumer substitution away from goods with high waste disposal costs towards those that will reduce the waste that households must ultimately pay to dispose of would in this way provide manufacturers with an incentive to change product design and packaging to reduce subsequent unnecessary waste.

However, it may be doubted whether in most cases the impact of waste charges at the efficient level would be sufficient to modify households' purchasing behaviour to any appreciable extent. The additional costs of waste disposal arising from the environmental taxes on disposal would represent a very small part of the price of any good; few consumers might therefore change their purchasing decisions, and consequently the incentive for producers to modify their products or packaging may be slight. Even where there are relatively cheap and cost-effective ways of reducing the environmental costs of waste disposal by changing the design and packaging of products, placing the price signals at the 'waste disposal' end of the chain from manufacturer to waste disposal may not give a sufficiently-clear price signal for these methods to be adopted by manufacturers.

As an alternative to levying new charges on waste disposal and relying on these to be transmitted back to manufacturers, it might be possible to introduce incentives at the 'manufacturer' end of the chain, by levying taxes on products and packaging that reflected the costs of their ultimate disposal. The level of the packaging tax on an individual product would be broadly the same as the waste disposal tax that would be levied on its disposal under the former system. The difference is that the incentive is felt directly by the manufacturer, rather than having to be transmitted back from waste disposal costs via households, and the incentive for manufacturers to switch to forms of packaging with lower disposal costs might thus be perceived more clearly by manufacturers. In addition, packaging taxes do not require an unbroken chain of financial linkages from waste disposal through households to manufacturer; the system would thus be compatible with the retention of non-volumetric charges for household waste disposal, where households face a zero marginal cost for disposal.[12]

National packaging taxes are not levied in either Britain or Germany, but some municipalities in Germany have shown interest in levying taxes on certain types of packaging. In particular, the city of Kassel introduced a packaging tax on disposable plates, cutlery and packaging for take-away food and drink in 1992. This measure was the subject of legal proceedings to challenge the power of the municipality to levy a tax in this form, but the recent outcome of this challenge has been to confirm that packaging taxes may be levied at municipal level, so long as similar taxes are not levied by the federal government. In the light of this judgement, further packaging tax initiatives may be developed by a number of other municipalities.

---

[12] Given the possibility that households might seek to avoid volumetric disposal charges by littering and other environmentally-damaging practices, there may be good reasons to collect household waste at zero marginal cost.

The Kassel tax applies to only one category of packaging. What would be required for a more comprehensive system of packaging taxes, to reflect the environmental costs of all types of packaging, if it is to provide an efficient structure of incentives for packaging choice and substitution between different types of packaging? Such a tax structure would require assumptions to be made about the form, and hence the environmental costs, of subsequent disposal for each type of product packaging. Products that were predominantly thrown away by households, ending up in landfills after one use, would be subject to a higher packaging tax than products that were recycled with lower environmental costs; both might be taxed more heavily than products packaged in reusable containers, for which the ultimate disposal costs would be divided by the number of times that they were reused.

Estimates by Brisson (1993) of the packaging tax on drinks containers that would internalise the disposal costs of each type of container suggest some surprising conclusions about the relative tax rates that should be applied to

TABLE 5.3

Calculation of packaging tax rates: an illustration based on UK data

	Recycling rate (%)	Weight (kg per 100l)	Packaging tax (pence per 100l)
PET bottle	5	3.00	6
Aluminium soft drink can (330ml)	8	5.15	9
Steel soft drink can (330ml)	10	8.48	15
Carton ('gable top' type)	0	2.90	6
Glass bottle (non-returnable, no recycling)	0	36.00	72
Glass bottle (93% reuse)	93	45.00	6

Note: Optimal packaging tax calculated as product of container weight per 100 litres, marginal disposal cost per tonne of packaging and (1 – the fraction recycled). Figures assume marginal collection and disposal costs of £20 per tonne throughout.
Source: Brisson, 1993.

drinks containers made of various different materials (Table 5.3). Cartons and plastic (PET) bottles, which are hardly recycled at all, would have low tax rates, because their weight and hence disposal costs are low. Nonreturnable glass bottles without recycling would have tax rates that were some 12 times as high as cartons and plastic containers. However, if sufficient rates of reuse and recycling are achieved, the tax rate for glass bottles falls sharply: at a 93 per cent rate of recycling, the tax rate for glass bottles has fallen to the level of the tax on cartons and plastic containers.

Packaging taxes of this form have been introduced for beverage containers and certain types of other packaging in some Scandinavian countries, and have been studied by Brisson (1993) and OECD (1993c). Neither the UK nor Germany currently appears to be considering use of such taxes. Instead, in Germany, a radically-different approach has been taken to establishing economic incentives for manufacturers and packagers to modify the form of product packaging, based on a reallocation of the responsibility for the costs of waste management from the public sector to private-sector manufacturers and packagers; aspects of this 'dual system' are also reflected in policy developments at the European level and within the UK.

5.4 The 'Dual System' in Germany

The 1986 Waste Management Act in Germany (Abfallgesetz) has provided the legal foundations for an innovative, and, to an extent, market-based, reorientation of German waste management policy. The Act gives the federal government the power to introduce further measures, or 'ordinances', which make the manufacturer of a particular product responsible for its whole life cycle, including its ultimate disposal. This approach effectively shifts the costs of waste management from municipalities to manufacturers, thereby providing manufacturers with an incentive to take the costs of later disposal into account in the design of products.

The first of the ordinances envisaged under the 1986 law, covering disposal of packaging waste (Verpackungsverordnung), was introduced in 1991. Others, making the producer of products such as cars, batteries, newspapers and magazines responsible for recycling and disposal, are under consideration.

The packaging ordinance defines three different categories of packaging, each of which is subject to particular requirements for reuse, recycling and disposal:

- 'primary' packaging, needed to protect and transport the product after purchase by final consumers;
- 'secondary' packaging, used in shops to protect products against theft or for advertising;
- 'transport' packaging, for protection of the product in transit from producer to sales outlet.

About four-fifths (by weight) of packaging material used in Germany is primary packaging, and one-fifth transport packaging; secondary packaging accounts for less than 1 per cent of the total (Klepper and Michaelis, 1995).

The ordinance requires that all transport packaging must be taken back for reuse or recycling, and that secondary packaging must be returned by retailers to the manufacturer. For primary packaging, the ordinance places an initial obligation on retailers to take back primary packaging and return it to manufacturers, and to operate deposit/refund systems for all containers of drinks, detergents and paints. The ordinance allows this onerous and costly obligation to be avoided, however, if producers instead organise a private collection and reprocessing system, parallel to the system of municipal waste collection, that achieves specified targets for collection and reprocessing (reuse or recycling) of the major categories of packaging waste.

In response to this option that the ordinance permits, a number of large retailers and packaging firms set up the parallel waste collection and disposal system Duales System Deutschland GmbH (DSD) in 1992. DSD aims to collect and sort primary packaging waste from households, and to arrange for reprocessing, so as to meet the minimum requirements for collection and reprocessing set out in the ordinance.

DSD's operations are financed by firms in the packaging industry, in two ways. First, a 'green dot' symbol identifies products that participate in the system, and packaging firms pay a licence fee to be allowed to use the green dot; this fee is set at a level intended to cover the costs of collection and sorting of household packaging waste. Subsequent reprocessing costs are then also borne by the packaging producers, who are required to contract for reprocessing of a given proportion of their packaging output; these reprocessing costs vary widely between packaging materials, since some can be recycled profitably whilst others (such as some plastics) are very costly to recycle. In the latter cases, large reprocessing costs have to be borne by producers, especially those making plastic packaging.

Participation in the dual system is voluntary, and the basic incentives needed for the system to function arise through the onerous obligation that retailers would otherwise bear to take back and return primary packaging, and to operate deposit/refund systems for many containers. Participation by manufacturers and packagers arises because of pressure from retailers. Major retailers and retailing groups have announced that, after a transition period, they will only sell products bearing the green dot; this has been sufficient to ensure that the vast majority of manufacturers use packaging from firms that take part in the scheme.

In establishing a system with such a radical reorientation of incentives, problems have naturally been encountered. These have included the destabilising impact that the increase in materials collected for recycling has had on the market for certain recycled materials (both in Germany and abroad), the difficulty of establishing adequate reprocessing capacity for certain types of plastic packaging, and the extremely high costs of reprocessing plastics more generally. Serious difficulties do not, however, appear to have been experienced at the household collection stage, where, although households are given no monetary incentive to sort packaging waste into the separate bins for collection by DSD, participation rates appear to have been high; as Michaelis (1995) observes, this is only likely to continue for as long as DSD can maintain a 'green' reputation, which in turn requires that the collected materials be reprocessed properly.

The system is intended to change behaviour towards a more environmentally-aware use of packaging, and a key yardstick in evaluating its performance must therefore be its impact on the volume and type of packaging employed by industry. All packaging is made more costly to manufacturers because of the 'green dot' fee covering collection costs. In addition, there will be differences between types of packaging in the extra costs incurred; for certain materials, such as some plastics, the reprocessing costs that packagers and manufacturers must bear will add substantially to the costs, by comparison with packaging that can be recycled profitably. Overall, Germany's use of primary and secondary packaging appears to have fallen by about one-tenth over the period since the dual system was introduced, with the greatest reductions being made in the use of glass and plastics.

Whilst the dual system establishes new incentives for manufacturers and packagers to take account of future waste disposal costs, and thus reflects an extension of the use of market incentives in environmental policy, it should be noted that the scope for market incentives to determine the final outcome is heavily constrained. Reuse and recycling targets are set for individual materials, and the relative costs of using different materials reflect the costs of meeting these targets, rather than the relative environmental costs of disposal of each type of material. As Klepper and Michaelis (1995) argue, this approach may lead to inefficient substitutions, if these targets do not correctly reflect the relative environmental costs of disposing of different materials. They favour, instead, the replacement of the targets for individual materials with environmental taxes on waste disposal and energy consumption, which would allow the amount of recycling of different materials within the dual system to be determined by reference to these underlying environmental costs, rather than by administratively-determined recycling targets.

Some of the key elements in the German dual system are reflected in European Union policy on packaging, and particularly in the EC Directive on Packaging and Packaging Waste (94/62/EC; *Official Journal of the European Communities*, no. L365, 31 December 1994), which came into force at the end of 1994. This requires member states to achieve recycling or recovery of between 50 and 65 per cent of packaging waste within five years. The British government's proposals for implementing the Directive have been the subject of a consultation exercise during 1995 (Department of the Environment, 1995). Various options for implementing 'producer responsibility' in packaging have been set out, differing principally in which firms (packaging material suppliers, product manufacturers, etc.) would bear the producer responsibility. As in Germany, the policy is based on quantitative targets for recovery of the different types of packaging, and whilst the policy would therefore harness an incentive mechanism to encourage producers to take account of disposal costs in the design of products, the balance between materials would be governed by the quantitative targets. As with the dual system, therefore, producer responsibility would use a reallocation of incentives to encourage changes in behaviour, but would limit the amount of flexibility possible in individual responses.

CHAPTER 6
Energy

Energy use raises a range of environmental issues — air pollution from smoky chimneys, sulphur dioxide and nitrogen oxides emissions causing acid rain, and emissions of carbon dioxide and other 'greenhouse gases' which may accelerate global warming. Of these, the last has attracted most attention in recent policy discussions, and has been the focus of a number of measures and proposals employing taxation as an environmental policy instrument.

This chapter considers three aspects of tax policy relating to energy use — the possible introduction of a carbon tax to reduce the risk of accelerated global warming, which has been proposed by the European Commission and extensively debated in both Britain and Germany, the environmental aspects of the taxation of domestic energy, over which there has recently been substantial domestic policy controversy in the UK, and the use of investment incentives in the corporate tax system, which might be used to stimulate greater investments in energy efficiency.

6.1 The Carbon Tax Debate

From the environmental point of view, the purpose of a carbon tax would be to reduce emissions of carbon dioxide (CO_2), one of the principal greenhouse gases. For this purpose, a tax in proportion to the carbon content of different fuels would be a well-linked incentive mechanism — CO_2 emissions from combustion are closely related to the carbon content of the fuels used, and the principal options for abatement of CO_2 emissions involve reductions in the carbon going into combustion processes, either through substitution to lower-carbon fuels or through reductions in the amount of fuel used. Unlike the problem of sulphur dioxide emissions from combustion, there is, at present, no cost-effective method of removing CO_2 from combustion emissions through end-of-pipe 'cleaning' technologies.

The scientific and environmental issues surrounding the carbon tax debate have been extensively researched, and the consensus developed through the work of the Intergovernmental Panel on Climate Change (IPCC) has been broadly accepted by governments as the basis for policy intervention. The environmental problem is that the accumulation of greenhouse gases in the atmosphere seems likely to lead to major climatic changes, probably including a rise in global temperatures, increased climatic volatility and climatic shifts affecting particular regions. Enormous uncertainty surrounds both the magnitude and timing of these climatic effects, and also the consequent economic costs and risks involved.

Measures to reduce greenhouse gas emissions would involve significant economic costs, and these can only be justified if they are exceeded by the costs of uncontrolled global warming (costs of sea-level rise and of climate changes causing changes in agriculture). What is the appropriate balance between adaptation (building sea walls and moving activities to reflect the change in climate patterns) and prevention?

Despite the great uncertainty, it may not be possible to postpone policy action until conclusive evidence has been obtained, without in the mean time risking irreversible changes in climate and in the global environment. Although it could turn out that gradual adaptation of the pattern of economic activity and human settlement might be far cheaper than prevention, the risk of catastrophic and irreversible climatic effects would justify some level of precautionary policy to restrict greenhouse gas emissions. Where policy measures can be taken that have low cost (including any 'no-regrets' measures), immediate action would avoid the risk of irreversible damage, whilst leaving the full range of policy options open, should future studies make major revisions to the scientific and economic assessments of the risks of global warming.

The context for British and German policy on carbon emissions is necessarily international. Since global warming is a function of global emissions, the impact on global warming of national policy in either Britain or Germany will be negligible unless measures with equivalent effect are taken by a large number of other countries.

International discussions have led to agreement amongst a large number of countries on the Global Convention on Climate Change, signed at Rio in 1992. This commits developed countries to taking the measures necessary to return their emissions of greenhouse gases to 1990 levels by the year 2000. Earlier, in October 1990, the European Community's joint Council of Energy and Environment Ministers had set a target for Community countries to stabilise emissions of CO_2, the main greenhouse gas, at 1990 levels by the year 2000. It requires a significant reduction of emissions compared with what otherwise would take place: without any policy action, EC estimates suggest that CO_2 emissions would rise by some 11 per cent over the period. The target of cutting emissions to 1990 levels by the year 2000 has also been adopted by the British government, whilst Germany has, in addition, committed itself to the more drastic goal of a 25 per cent reduction of CO_2 emissions compared with a 1987 base level by the year 2005.

As part of the Community's response to the environmental problem of global warming, the European Commission proposed in September 1991 the introduction of a Community-wide carbon/energy tax. The tax, which would have been introduced in stages, starting at the equivalent of $3 per barrel of oil in 1993 and increasing by $1 per barrel annually, to $10 per barrel of oil in the year 2000, would have been a two-part tax, reflecting both the carbon and energy content of fuel. Fossil fuels such as

FIGURE 6.1

Carbon dioxide content per unit of energy of different fuels

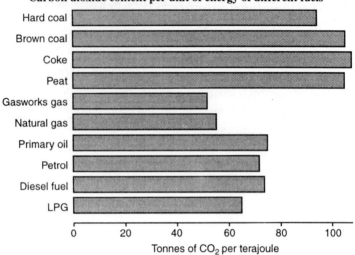

Source: Commission of the European Communities, DG II.

gas, coal and oil would bear a tax comprising two components, one related to their carbon content (Figure 6.1), the other related to their energy content. Non-renewable forms of energy other than fossil fuels (mainly nuclear power) would be subject to the energy-related part of the tax, but would not bear the carbon component. The tax rates per tonne of carbon and per joule of energy would have been set so that on a barrel of oil the carbon and energy components would have been weighted 50:50.

According to Commission estimates (Table 6.1) of the price impact of the proposed tax at its final level, the price of fuels used by industry would have increased by between 30 per cent (gas) and 60 per cent (coal). Domestic fuel prices would have risen on average by some 15 per cent. Because of its high price per unit of energy, reflecting high existing taxes and processing and distribution costs, the price of petrol would have risen by only 6 per cent.

The tax revenues would accrue to the member states of the Community, not to the EC budget. Member states

TABLE 6.1

Commission estimates of the percentage increase in fuel prices, based on a $10 per barrel carbon/energy tax, fully passed on to the energy user

		Per cent
Power-stations and industry	Hard coal	58
	Heavy fuel oil	45
	Natural gas	34
Households	Light fuel oil	16
	Natural gas	14
Transport	Petrol	6
	Diesel	11

Source: Commission of the European Communities, 1991, Annex 7.

would thus have been able to determine the use to be made of the revenues, although the Commission was at pains to stress that the introduction of the carbon/energy tax should be accompanied by reductions in other taxes, rather than by increases in public expenditures.

After an extensive amount of discussion between the Commission and the member states in both economic and environmental policy committees, it proved impossible to reach agreement to implement the carbon/energy tax proposal. The UK was implacably opposed — as an issue of principle — to the extension of the Community's mandate in the field of taxation which a Community agreement on co-ordinated introduction of a carbon/energy tax would have involved, and some other member states had considerable reservations about other aspects of the proposal, notably the likely impact on industrial costs and competitiveness. Towards the end of 1994, the draft Directive was withdrawn, although discussion continued about an alternative Directive which would provide a 'framework' to govern the structure of carbon taxes which individual member states might choose to introduce. Essentially, the initiative on carbon taxes has now returned to the member

TABLE 6.2

**Electricity production in Germany and the UK,
by source of energy used for generation, 1989 and 1993**

Per cent

	West Germany, 1989	Germany, 1993	UK, 1989	UK, 1993
Hydroelectric and geothermal	4.6	4.2	2.2	2.3
Nuclear	34.3	30.2	21.7	23.1
Coal	47.7	54.5	66.4	62.2
Oil	2.5	2.4	7.5	8.6
Gas	9.9	7.8	1.8	3.3
Other conventional	1.0	1.0	0.4	0.4

Note: Columns do not necessarily add to 100 due to rounding.
Source: EUROSTAT, *Energy Yearly Statistics 1992*, pp. 114–15.

states; co-ordinated, Community-wide, carbon taxation seems unlikely, at least in the short term.

As far as the relatively short-term commitments made at Rio to reduce CO_2 emissions are concerned, both Britain and Germany appear likely to experience significant reductions in emissions from at least some sources without additional tax measures. In Britain's case, a severe economic recession reduced the rate of growth of energy demand during the early 1990s, and the privatisation of the electricity industry has led to a massive switch in the fuels used for electricity generation from coal to gas.[13] As a result, although the government has not been able to implement all of the package of measures initially proposed as part of its strategy to reach the Rio target, Britain looks set to achieve its target for the year 2000 quite

---

[13] Table 6.2 shows the gas share beginning to rise, between 1989 and 1993, but the full effects of recent investments in gas-fired generation capacity had still to feed through into the pattern of fuel use.

comfortably. Likewise, Germany finds itself in a position where economic changes can be expected to contribute large reductions in CO_2 emissions from certain sources without any policy intervention; in particular, the wave of plant closures in heavy industry in the former GDR which has followed reunification, and improvements in energy efficiency in those plants that remain,[14] mean that substantial emission reductions across Germany as a whole are likely to be achieved.

Nevertheless, over a longer time horizon, continuing restraint in CO_2 emissions is likely to require a more coherent and far-reaching intervention in private-sector patterns of energy use. In this context, there are considerable advantages to the cost-minimising property of using taxes rather than regulation to induce private-sector energy savings. The debate about carbon taxation is thus likely to continue.

Three key issues seem likely to dominate future policy decisions about carbon taxation:

- Concerns about the impact of carbon taxes on industry's costs and international competitiveness have figured prominently in industry's response to the EC proposal. The Commission suggested various measures to try to limit the impact of the tax on industrial competitiveness, including exemptions for energy-intensive industries and firms; for the same reason, it was decided at an early stage in the discussion that the European tax should not be introduced unless similar measures were taken by other major industrial countries. Likewise, in those countries, such as Sweden, that have introduced carbon taxes on a unilateral basis, application of the tax to

---

[14] Although these effects are partly offset by the very rapid rise in energy use for road transport in the new Länder.

industry has tended to be limited by competitiveness concerns; the Swedish carbon tax was modified soon after its introduction to reduce sharply the level of taxation on industrial energy use.

It should be observed that, as far as the long-run economic effects of a carbon tax are concerned, the question of the impact on competitiveness is predominantly an issue concerning the relative impact on different industries, rather than concerning overall industrial competitiveness. Indefinite disequilibrium in the balance of payments, in which all domestic industries are permanently disadvantaged in international competition by the imposition of a carbon tax, is not a feasible situation; at some point, economic adjustments that would restore the balance of payments to equilibrium would have to take place. These could take the form either of exchange rate changes or of changes in the domestic wage and price level, which would offset the impact of the carbon tax on the prices of domestically-produced goods in international trade. On average, therefore, the higher energy costs may be offset by a subsequent exchange-rate adjustment, and whilst energy-intensive industries would experience a loss of competitiveness, those sectors that are less energy-intensive would gain.

- More generally than the issue of trade competitiveness, there has been a lengthy debate about the extent to which a shift in the burden of taxation from existing tax bases to energy, or carbon, might be expected to lead to economic as well as environmental gains. Macro-economic modelling of the economic impact of such a reform (including Bach, Kohlhaas and Praetorius (1994) for Germany and Barker, Baylis and Bryden (1994) for the UK) has indicated a wide range of possible effects, and has suggested that there may be circumstances in which a tax reform of this sort would actually confer economic gains, in terms of either increased GDP or increased employment, compared with a baseline case in which revenues were raised through the existing tax system. Nevertheless, the issue remains highly controversial amongst economists, in particular because theoretical analysis suggests that the scope for a genuine 'double dividend', in terms of both environmental benefits and a lower welfare cost of raising tax revenues, may well be very limited (Goulder, 1995).

• A third issue, which has been especially prominent in the UK debate about the taxation of energy, concerns the distributional impact of the tax payments. In the UK, spending on household energy for heating forms a considerable proportion of total spending by households in the poorest income groups, and domestic energy spending rises little with increasing income. Taxes on domestic energy spending are therefore sharply regressive, an observation that played a decisive role in opposition to the government's plans to extend

TABLE 6.3

Carbon tax payments,
by decile and quartile groups of gross household income

	Germany *(ECUs per annum)*	UK *(ECUs per annum)*	Germany *(% of total household spending)*	UK *(% of total household spending)*
All households	146	161	0.86	1.19
Decile groups				
Poorest 10%	62	94	1.06	2.58
Second 10%	84	115	1.01	2.03
Third 10%	100	128	0.96	1.74
Quartile groups				
Poorest 25%	77	108	1.01	2.10
Second 25%	124	145	0.94	1.45
Third 25%	165	173	0.87	1.16
Richest 25%	218	219	0.77	0.92

Source: Smith, 1992b.

standard-rate VAT to domestic energy (see Section 6.2). The distributional incidence of a carbon tax would, however, be less regressive than taxes on domestic energy spending alone, since the carbon tax would also apply to motor fuels, which are not a large part of the spending of the poorest income groups, and also to industrial energy use (and, if passed on in prices, this component would be broadly proportionate to household non-energy spending). The estimates shown in Table 6.3, drawn from Smith (1992b), suggest that the European carbon tax would have had a markedly greater regressive distributional impact in the UK than in Germany. Quite apart from this difference in the objective situation in the two countries, it also appears clear that the issue of the distributional effects of the carbon/energy tax has had much greater political resonance in the UK than in Germany; in Germany, other issues have dominated the carbon tax debate.

FIGURE 6.2

Carbon tax payments as a percentage of total household expenditures, by quartile groups of gross household income

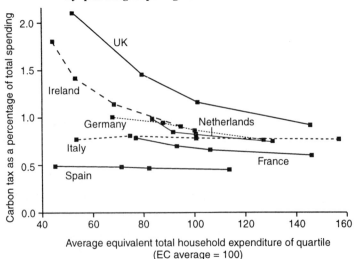

6.2 VAT on Domestic Energy in Britain

A decision to impose VAT on domestic energy was announced in the March 1993 Budget. Along with food, public transport, water supplies, children's clothes, and books and newspapers, domestic energy had previously been zero-rated for VAT in the UK. The March 1993 Budget set a timetable for the extension of VAT to domestic energy, to be phased over two years. An 8 per cent rate of VAT was applied to sales of energy to households from 1 April 1994, and this was then to have been increased to the standard 17.5 per cent VAT rate from 1 April 1995.

The main motivation for extending the standard rate of VAT to include domestic energy was the search for additional sources of tax revenue that could help to close a substantial medium-term gap between government revenues and expenditures. By the time of the March 1993 Budget, the public sector borrowing requirement (PSBR) for the fiscal year 1992–93 had reached £40 billion, and, on unchanged policies, was then forecast to exceed £50 billion in 1993–94 (8.75 per cent of GDP) and to continue at roughly this level in the medium term, even allowing for economic growth at 3 per cent per annum. The phased imposition of VAT on domestic energy was one of a number of measures included in the March 1993 and November 1993 Budgets to increase projected revenues in future years. Charging VAT on domestic fuels was predicted in the Financial Statement and Budget Report (FSBR) to raise £950 million in 1994–95, £2.3 billion in 1995–96 and around £3 billion annually thereafter (HM Treasury, 1993).

The extension of VAT in 1994–95 related to domestic energy only; to conform with European Community requirements (which permit zero-rating only where there is a justification in terms of social policy objectives), supplies of energy to non-domestic users had been subject to VAT since July 1990.

Environmental considerations were not the primary reason for imposing VAT on domestic energy. However, government statements noted two environmental dimensions of the policy:

- Firstly, it was suggested that the imposition of VAT on domestic energy should be seen as an alternative to the implementation of the European Commission's proposed carbon/energy tax. VAT on domestic energy increases the price of domestic fuels in the UK by roughly the same percentage, on average, as would result from imposition of a $10 per barrel carbon tax, although the relative burden of the tax differs, with VAT bearing less heavily on carbon-intensive fuels such as coal than the carbon tax, and more heavily on low-carbon fuels. Also, unlike the proposed carbon tax, VAT does not provide any incentive for changes in industrial energy use.
- Secondly, imposition of standard-rate VAT on domestic energy would remove a source of perverse incentives in the VAT system. While domestic energy was zero-rated, investments in energy-efficiency measures (loft and wall insulation, double glazing, etc.) had been subject to the standard rate of VAT; the tax system thus acted to increase the costs of such investments relative to the benefits, and hence to discourage domestic energy-efficiency investment.

Opposition to the ending of VAT zero-rating centred on the impact of higher energy prices on the budgets of poor and especially elderly households, and on the risk that some vulnerable groups, especially the elderly, might be unable to afford adequate heating. Analysis by Crawford, Smith and Webb (1993) of the distributional issue showed that whilst the initial distributional impact of the tax was clearly regressive, there was, in fact, considerable scope for policy measures that would alleviate much of

TABLE 6.4

Simulation of the effects on household energy spending and indirect
tax payments of imposing VAT on domestic energy at 17.5 per cent
(Great Britain, 1991 basis)

	Additional indirect tax payments (£ p.w.)	Additional indirect tax payments, as a percentage of total spending	Percentage change in consumption of domestic energy
All households	£2.06	1.1%	−5.8%
Quintile of net equivalent household income			
Poorest	£1.56	2.0%	−9.2%
Second	£1.83	1.3%	−8.3%
Third	£2.11	0.9%	−6.2%
Fourth	£2.18	0.7%	−4.2%
Richest	£2.63	0.6%	−1.1%

Source: Crawford, Smith and Webb, 1993, p. 21.

the distributional problem. Some part of the revenues raised from the VAT could be used to pay increased means-tested benefits and pensions, leaving the most vulnerable groups able to afford as much energy as before the measure was introduced; indeed, indexation of benefit rates would ensure that benefit levels reflected higher fuel costs automatically, albeit with a time lag. There was also scope for using some of the revenues to finance measures to stimulate greater standards of domestic energy efficiency; since the poor insulation standards of much British housing are the root cause of the high levels of energy spending by poor households, measures to tackle market failures in energy efficiency might confer both efficiency improvements and a reduction in the distributional obstacles to efficient energy pricing.

A vocal campaign of protest against the ending of VAT zero-rating led the government in November 1994 to abandon its plans for the second-stage rise in the VAT rate, to the full standard rate, from April 1995. VAT on domestic energy thus remains at a rate of 8 per cent, and further increases in the rate are extremely unlikely. The environmental gains from the ending of VAT zero-rating have been correspondingly reduced by the abandonment of the second stage of the policy. Whilst an overall reduction of domestic energy use of some 6 per cent might have been expected from the imposition of standard rate VAT (Crawford, Smith and Webb, 1993), this will have been roughly halved by the decision to keep the rate at 8 per cent. In addition, the non-neutrality in VAT treatment between, on the one hand, domestic energy spending and, on the other, energy-efficiency materials and investments remains in place, albeit somewhat reduced in size.

6.3   Tax Incentives for Energy-Efficiency Investments

In addition to taxes on emissions, environmental tax policies might make use of corporate tax incentives such as accelerated depreciation for pollution-abatement investments. Taxes and tax incentives might be used together to increase the responsiveness of polluters to pollution-abatement incentives. Whilst such an approach might be adopted for a number of pollution problems, perhaps the most obvious practical application would be to encourage energy-efficiency investments.

In Germany, accelerated depreciation provisions in the income tax law had, until the start of 1991, been available for investments in capital equipment with a substantial environmental purpose, including equipment for reducing air pollution, waste water discharges, noise, vibrations and waste. Investments in capital equipment qualified for the accelerated depreciation if the pollution-abatement aspect of the investment counted for at least 70 per cent of the value of the investment. On these investments, accelerated depreciation of up to 60 per cent was permitted in the fiscal year when the capital equipment was purchased or constructed, followed by depreciation at the rate of 10 per cent annually thereafter until the investment was fully amortised. This compares with straight-line depreciation rates applied to fixed investments in general of some 10–12 per cent.[15]

Similar provisions for accelerated depreciation on investments in energy efficiency have also recently been abolished in Germany. Until the end of 1991, building alterations intended to reduce energy use or to promote use of renewable energy, including thermal insulation and the installation of environmentally-favourable heating systems such as district heating, heat pumps and systems using solar and wind energy, qualified for accelerated depreciation on purchase or construction costs of up to 10 per cent in the first fiscal year and each of the subsequent nine years.[16]

A number of other OECD countries operate similar systems of investment incentives for categories of pollution-control expenditure (OECD, 1993b). The UK, however, does not have such measures, despite its past extensive experience of using more-general systems of investment incentives. More generally, such measures run counter to much of the general policy trend in corporate taxation, which is to aim for a broadly neutral tax system without special incentives favouring particular activities or investments.

What are the issues involved in employing corporate tax incentives to encourage greater investment in

---

[15] In 1985, the provisions were applied to investments to a total value of some DM3,800 million, and it was estimated that in that year the accelerated depreciation provision reduced public revenues by some DM480 million (Rodi, 1993a and 1993b). Aggregate corporate profits tax revenues in 1985 were DM42,500 million.

[16] The provisions were estimated to involve an annual revenue loss of some DM500 billion.

pollution-control measures, along the lines of the system recently in operation in Germany? Such tax incentives for investment could take a number of forms, but may be divided into two broad categories — those (such as various forms of accelerated depreciation) that operate by postponing tax payments, thus reducing the discounted net present value of tax payments, and those (such as investment tax credits) that reduce the undiscounted total of tax payments.

Whilst corporate tax incentives are delivered through the tax system, it is important to be clear that what they involve is, in essence, the payment of subsidy, compared with the 'baseline' tax system. The tax system merely provides a convenient way of paying the subsidy. The issues raised by tax incentives are thus, primarily, those raised by the use of pollution-abatement subsidies more generally. A second, and subsidiary, issue is whether subsidy should be paid directly or through the tax system.

Theoretical analysis of the relative merits of pollution-abatement subsidy and pollution taxes indicates that taxes would normally be preferable to policy measures based on subsidy. This is for two main reasons.

- Subsidies may not lead to the optimal level of rationalisation in polluting industries; pollution-abatement subsidies maintain the profits of polluting firms at a higher level than do pollution taxes, and thus may encourage too many polluting firms to remain active in polluting industries. In some cases, subsidy may even *increase* rather than reduce aggregate pollution.
- Subsidies involve public expenditure, and hence require taxes to be raised to pay for them; environmental taxes, on the other hand, raise revenue, and thus permit other taxes to be reduced.

In modifying the existing fiscal system to strengthen environmental incentives, it will therefore generally be more efficient to tax emissions than to subsidise pollution abatement, either directly or through tax incentives. However, it may not always be feasible, for either administrative or political reasons, to rely wholly on taxing polluters. In some cases, the level of taxes required will be very high. Powerful polluter lobbies may resist being required to pay for what they had previously regarded as an implicit property right to a given level of emissions. Governments may be unwilling to accept the shift in international competitiveness that could arise when high environmental taxes are levied on industrial processes. Social and distributional considerations, too, may require moderation in the taxation of polluting necessities — such as domestic energy, perhaps. And, in some cases, the levels of taxation required may in practice be unenforceable or may provide undesirably-high incentives for evasion. All of these arguments suggest that it may not be possible to set pollution taxes at a level as high as the first-best policy would require.

If policy is constrained to employ only relatively-modest environmental taxes, subsidies may have a role to play. In this context, it is possible to argue for the use of pollution-abatement investment subsidies (or tax incentives), as a possible complement to pollution-abatement incentives based on modest, constrained, environmental taxes. The point of such a combined use of instruments is that the investment subsidies may play a role in increasing the elasticity of response to the limited environmental tax. The combination of investment subsidy plus tax may induce greater change in polluting behaviour than could be achieved through the use of the tax alone.

The issues raised by tax incentives and other abatement subsidies include:

- *Potential effectiveness.* Tax incentives are only likely to stimulate abatement investment in certain circumstances. Where the investment simply reduces pollution levels, without providing the investing firm with any other benefits, subsidising part of the cost would not be likely to have any impact on firms' decisions. However, if pollution-control investments reduce private costs or confer private gains, perhaps in the form of materials recovery, as well as reducing the social costs of pollution, subsidy might then increase the level of investment. In addition, a combined package, involving both subsidy and emissions taxation, could be effective, even where subsidy alone would fail, since the emissions taxation would provide the firm with a private benefit from reduced emissions.

- *Evidence on effectiveness.* Experience with more-general investment incentives suggests that the effects of a subsidy on investment levels might be quite modest. Studies of general investment incentives paid through the tax system in the US and the UK during the 1970s and 1980s do not suggest that the effects have been large (see, for example, Bond, Denny and Devereux (1992)). Some effect, however, was found of the very large, and temporary, incentive that arose during the reform of the UK corporate tax system in 1984. However, not all of this experience may be relevant to the case of tax incentives for pollution-abatement investments: for these to work, a firm's tax and technology decisions need to be more closely integrated than is usual in existing business practice.
- *Implementation.* The difficulties of distinguishing between the qualifying and ineligible components of major investment projects would be formidable, and potentially a source of distortion and inefficiency in firms' pollution-abatement technology choices.
- *Limiting public expenditure costs.* It may be possible to limit the public expenditure costs of subsidies, to some extent at least, by restricting eligibility to only those investments that would not be undertaken in the absence of the subsidy. Such tests of 'additionality' try

to avoid paying subsidies to projects that would have gone ahead anyway, but face considerable problems of information and implementation.

- *Transparency.* Subsidies paid through the tax system undermine efficiency and accountability in public decision-making, if the amounts paid are not explicitly shown in public budget statements. A number of countries, including the UK, now make regular statements of the public expenditure equivalent of 'tax expenditure' provisions within the tax system, to try to improve the transparency of public decision-making.

- *Compatibility with the 'Polluter Pays Principle' (PPP).* Whilst incentives for pollution-control investments paid through the direct tax system are, in most cases, formally compatible with the PPP — an international agreement supervised by the OECD on the form of pollution-control policies — they clearly depart from the spirit of the PPP, which has aimed to outlaw environmental policy subsidies to prevent such subsidies being used as an indirect means of trade protection. The PPP plays an important role in preserving the credibility of trade policy institutions, and policy changes that might undermine the clarity of the PPP may have wider economic costs which should be taken into account.

CHAPTER 7
Transport

Road transport provides considerable opportunities for enhancing the environmental orientation of the tax system in both Britain and Germany. Road transport is already heavily taxed through taxes levied on motor vehicles and on motor fuels, so that there is plenty of scope for introducing environmental incentives by restructuring these existing taxes rather than establishing wholly-new 'green' taxes or charges.

Formulating efficient environmental tax policies for road transport is, however, complex, because of the range of social costs involved and because of the complex interactions between road transport, other modes of transport and issues of spatial development. In general, road transport taxes can reflect the various externalities only approximately, and optimal policy will therefore need to employ both tax and non-tax instruments in combination.

In principle, the taxation of road transport might be used to address each of the principal forms of social cost involved in vehicle use:

- environmental costs including global and local air pollution, noise and aesthetic losses;
- congestion costs and accident costs imposed on other road users; and
- the otherwise-uncharged costs of consumption of publicly-provided road infrastructure.

It is desirable that these social costs should be reflected in the costs of road use faced by individual road users. The tax system may have an important role to play in achieving this. In practice, policymakers have often been unclear about which — if any — of the various social costs is reflected in the high level of taxation on motor vehicles and vehicle fuels.

Whilst the ideal policy might be for road users to be charged the full marginal social cost of vehicle use, it is not possible to restructure existing taxes on vehicles or fuels so as to achieve exactly the ideal structure of incentives. The various environmental costs differ in how closely they are related to the characteristics of vehicles or fuels. Some, such as the global warming potential of vehicle use, are closely (and broadly linearly) related to fuel consumption. Others, including the costs of smog-inducing emissions, particulate emissions and noise, are related to the location, and in some cases the time of day, of vehicle use. Fuel taxes would be a poor proxy for these components of the environmental costs.

The existing taxes on road transport in Britain and Germany include those levied on vehicle purchase and initial registration, annual charges on vehicle use, and taxes on motor fuels. In addition, the tax system contains provisions relating to car use for commuting and to subsidised or free car provision by employers to their employees. Each of these aspects of motor taxation might in principle affect the environmental externalities arising from road transport. The six subsequent sections discuss various policy options for environmentally-motivated reforms to the level and structure of existing road transport taxes.

7.1 Taxes on Motor Vehicle Purchase and Registration

Vehicle ownership, and hence the aggregate level of vehicle use, may be affected by taxes on the sale and registration of new motor vehicles and by recurrent (e.g. annual) taxes on vehicle ownership or use.

As far as taxes on the sale of vehicles are concerned, both Britain and Germany impose VAT at the standard

TABLE 7.1

Number of motor vehicles per 1,000 inhabitants

	Germany	UK
1970	250	243
1990	517	420

Source: EUROSTAT, *Transport Statistics 1990*.

rate on new cars (17.5 per cent in Britain, 15 per cent in Germany). For many years, Britain had also imposed an additional 'car tax' at 10 per cent on five-sixths of the list price of a new car. This was halved to 5 per cent in March 1992, and fully-abolished in November 1992, mainly in response to pressure from the motor vehicle industry, which was at the time experiencing a slump in the level of new car sales.

In Britain, an annual lump-sum tax in the form of vehicle excise duty (VED) of £135 is levied on the use of a private car. For some years (1985–91), this tax had been held constant in nominal terms at £100, whilst at the same time the excise taxes on motor fuels were raised broadly in pace with inflation, with the aim of shifting the balance of motor taxes from taxes on ownership to taxes on use. However, since 1992, annual Budgets have again included increases in VED.

In Germany, the annual motor vehicle tax on vehicles licensed for use on public roads has been structured to provide a tax incentive for 'clean' cars (cars meeting EU emissions standards). The annual tax rate for low-emission cars is DM13.20 per 100cc, whilst for cars not meeting the low-emission criteria, different rates apply depending on the age of the vehicle. For cars registered before 1986, the tax rate per 100cc is DM18.80, and for cars registered in 1986 or later, it is DM21.60.[17] Higher rates of motor vehicle tax apply to diesel-engined cars: since the start of 1994, these have been taxed at the petrol car rates plus DM23.90 per 100cc. Earlier, additional tax incentives had been employed to accelerate the take-up of catalytic converters, ahead of the requirements stipulated in European Union legislation on vehicle emissions (Blum and Rottengatter, 1990).

In both countries, the taxes levied on commercial vehicle sales, ownership and use are higher and more complex than the taxes on private cars, reflecting the greater variety in size and use amongst commercial vehicles, and the impact of commercial vehicle taxes on the competitiveness of the national road haulage industry. In the UK, the VED on commercial freight vehicles is substantially higher than that on cars, and is related to the number of axles and vehicle weight. In Germany, the weight-related motor vehicle tax on lorries was to have been replaced by a tax related to weight, the number of axles and annual mileage, so as to increase the accuracy with which the tax proxies road-use costs; however, this measure was suspended following a European Court ruling that its application to foreign-registered vehicles could have adverse effects on competition within the European market.

From the environmental point of view, the taxes on purchase and use of motor vehicles raise a number of issues. They may potentially affect the level of car ownership, the age composition of the motor vehicle stock, and the aggregate amount of use made of motor vehicles.

- The level of annual taxation on motor vehicles, such as the UK's VED, has its primary effect on the level of vehicle ownership. Whilst these taxes are, in general, small in relation to the total costs of annual car ownership (depreciation, insurance, maintenance and running

---

[17] To illustrate the scale of the differential taxation, the owner of a car with a 1,500cc engine would pay DM198 p.a. (£89) if meeting the low-emission criteria; otherwise, the tax would be DM282 p.a. (£126) if the car were registered before 1986 and DM324 (£145) if registered after 1986.

costs), they would presumably be an influence on ownership decisions at the margin. In turn, however, ownership will affect aggregate use: once a household has taken the decision to own a car, the marginal cost of journeys is low, and the car will tend to be used, even if the aggregate net benefit the household derives from car ownership is little greater than that from non-ownership.

It is sometimes argued that, from an environmental point of view, it would be better to concentrate the burden of motoring taxes on taxes relating to the amount of car use (such as fuel taxes) rather than on the costs of car ownership (e.g. VED), since it is vehicle use rather than ownership that gives rise to most of the environmental problems from private motoring. With an ideal tax treatment of all aspects of transport, this argument has some strength. However, it can be seen that a switch in the balance of motoring taxes of this sort (as implemented to a limited extent in the UK over 1985–91) could conceivably *increase* the level of vehicle use, if the impact on car-ownership levels (and consequent additional vehicle use by 'new' car owners) outweighs any reduction in car use by existing vehicle owners in response to the higher fuel taxes.

- Annual taxes might have a particular effect on the ownership of very old cars, which might already be of marginal value to their owners. Higher annual taxes might thus accelerate the scrapping of old cars. The emissions per mile of old cars tend to be higher than those of the vehicle stock on average, because old cars tend to have been built to less stringent emissions standards than new cars and because emissions performance tends to decline as vehicles become older. It is worth noting that some European countries have introduced fiscal incentives for accelerated scrapping of old motor vehicles.[18] In both Germany and the UK, however, retirement of old vehicles is largely governed by stringent annual roadworthiness tests, in which emissions performance is now one of the required performance criteria.

- The level of taxes on new vehicle purchase could also have effects both on the level of vehicle ownership and on the average age of the vehicle stock. The impact on average vehicle age would arise through the influx of new vehicles to the vehicle stock, and possible consequent adjustments to second-hand vehicle prices and ownership decisions throughout the vehicle stock. If new cars become cheaper, second-hand cars become less valuable, and, at the margin, some may again be scrapped. The environmental impact of the additional sales of new vehicles could thus include both desirable and undesirable effects, reflecting both the environmental costs incurred in the manufacture of new cars and the lower level of use and accelerated scrapping of old cars.

- Both initial sales taxes and annual taxes on cars could be differentiated to induce substitution to less-polluting cars, either by differentiating the tax according to characteristics that proxy emissions levels (e.g. engine size) or by basing the tax on direct measurements of emissions performance from existing vehicles. This option has not been pursued in the UK for motor cars, where VED is an equal lump sum for all cars, but Germany has operated differential taxes of the first sort for many years, and has now moved towards taxes based on the emissions performance of particular vehicle types. Either would be straightforward to introduce in the UK VED system, and a recent report of the Royal Commis-

---

[18] Similar incentives arise in parts of the US, where utilities may be permitted to fulfil some of their environmental obligations by buying up and scrapping highly-polluting vehicles (Alberini, Edelstein, Harrington and McConnell, 1994).

sion on Environmental Pollution (1994) has argued that
VED in the UK should become steeply graduated and
based on the fuel efficiency standard achieved by the
vehicle when new.

A more ambitious measure would be to base annual
taxes on direct measurement of the emissions performance of each individual vehicle (e.g. in the annual
roadworthiness test) and perhaps also on recorded
mileage. This would clearly be a much closer measure
of the environmental impact, but would, however, introduce considerably greater administrative complexity and some risk of fraudulent measurement.

7.2   Increasing the Level of Motor Fuel Taxes

Motor fuels are taxed heavily in both Britain and Germany, and raise substantial tax revenues. In 1990, motor
fuel taxes accounted for 5 per cent of total tax revenues in
the UK and for 4 per cent in Germany. These taxes include
both a specific excise duty upon motor fuels, in the form
of a fixed amount per litre of fuel, and standard-rate VAT
applied over and above the excise duty. Table 7.2 shows
the rates of motor fuel excise applying in Germany and
the UK.

Both Britain and Germany have implemented substantial increases in motor fuel excises in recent years. In
Britain, the government has made a commitment, as part

TABLE 7.2

Excise duties on motor fuels in Britain and Germany

	Germany, 1994 (DM per litre)	Germany, 1994 (pence per litre)	UK from April 1995 (pence per litre)
Petrol (leaded)	1.08	43.53	36.10
Petrol (unleaded)	0.98	39.50	31.30
Diesel	0.62	24.99	31.30
LPG	0.31	12.49	12.93

of its strategy to curb greenhouse gas emissions, to a steady annual increase in motor fuel duties, of 3 per cent in real terms. In Germany, the excise duty on petrol doubled in nominal terms between 1986 and 1994, representing a rise in real terms of some 60 per cent, both for reasons of environmental policy and, since 1990, as part of the measures taken to finance the public expenditures involved in reunification.

Higher petrol prices would, in principle, have three main effects of relevance to environmental policy objectives:

- *Reductions in vehicle use.* The cost of each journey made would increase, and 'marginal' or inessential journeys would be discouraged.
- *Reductions in vehicle ownership.* For some owners of motor vehicles, a higher petrol price would make ownership no longer worth while. The number of vehicles owned would fall, as a result of fewer purchases of new vehicles and/or earlier scrapping of existing vehicles.
- *Higher fuel efficiency of the vehicle stock.* Higher petrol prices would tend to encourage manufacturers to design more fuel-efficient motor vehicles, and to encourage purchasers of new cars to choose more fuel-efficient vehicles. Also, high petrol prices might encourage the more rapid scrapping of 'gas-guzzling' older vehicles.

Most of the available econometric evidence on the impact of changes in motor fuel taxation concerns the 'own-price' relationship between the price of petrol and petrol consumption. The consensus in OECD countries is that this is quite low in the short term, although of considerably greater significance over a longer period of time. According to the European Commission's survey of petrol consumption elasticities with respect to price from 1966 to 1975 (Commission of the European Communities,

1980), 'There is substantial evidence to support a short run one year elasticity of about –0.2'. It also found that the minimum long-term elasticity is 'approximately –0.4 or twice that of the short term'. This conclusion is strengthened by Goodwin's later survey (1992), based on data for a wide range of countries, which concluded that 'there is a reasonably clear pattern for long term elasticities to be between 50% and three times higher than the short term'.

The above evidence relates to the effects of motor fuel price changes on fuel consumption, and thus provides a guide to the likely impact of policies to increase fuel prices on the externalities associated with fuel consumption, such as the level of greenhouse gas emissions from motoring. To the extent that these reductions in fuel consumption occur because fewer journeys are made, there will also be an effect on the externalities relating to vehicle use, such as accidents and congestion. However, the effect of petrol prices on traffic levels is likely to be less than that on petrol consumption, due to the scope for increases in fuel efficiency through changes in driving behaviour and, in the long run, the purchase of more fuel-efficient new vehicles.

Higher taxation of motor fuels has distributional effects, in terms of a differential impact on different groups in the population. Given the substantial increases in tax levels that will be implied by the steady 3 per cent real rise in motor fuel excise in the UK, for example, the distributional impact may be of some significance.

The distributional impact of changes in motor fuel taxes in the UK has been discussed by Johnson, McKay and Smith (1990), using simulation results from a consumer demand model estimated using UK household micro-data. The distributional effects of the petrol tax increase across the income distribution as a whole are relatively modest. Petrol spending tends to increase with income at lower income levels, because the density of car ownership is much lower amongst low-income house-

TABLE 7.3

Percentage of households with cars, across areas with different population density: all households, and bottom 30 per cent of income distribution, UK, 1986

	Percentage of all households with cars		Percentage of households in bottom 30 per cent of income distribution with cars	
London	58.5	(94)	18.7	(83)
Other metropolitan areas	52.0	(83)	14.4	(64)
Rural areas, high density	62.1	(99)	23.2	(103)
Rural areas, medium density	69.4	(111)	23.8	(105)
Rural areas, low density	70.6	(113)	34.4	(152)
Average, all households	62.5	(100)	22.6	(100)

Note: Figures in parentheses show car ownership as a percentage of the average across all areas.
Source: Johnson, McKay and Smith, 1990.

holds (Table 7.3). The additional petrol duty therefore has a progressive distributional incidence across income groups, in the sense of taking a higher percentage of spending from better-off households. Unlike the case of tax increases on domestic energy, the changes in the distribution of tax payments across the income distribution as a whole as a result of higher petrol taxes raise no obvious distributional issues.

Nevertheless, as Pearson and Smith (1990) note, high taxes on petrol may — in the short term, at least — be unacceptable for their impact on certain groups, such as rural dwellers, for whom no alternatives to petrol consumption may be available in the short term. Such households may have high consumption, and, unlike urban dwellers, may not easily be able to switch to public transport. In the long run, of course, household location decisions provide a further route by which individual households may respond to higher fuel prices; over a period of a number of years, higher fuel taxes may affect the pattern of residential location, as households move to areas that support a public transport service. However, in the shorter term, increases in petrol duty may lead to unavoidable increases in the tax burden on poorer rural households, without having any significant impact on their fuel consumption.

7.3   Tax Treatment of 'Company Cars'

In both Britain and Germany, cars provided by employers to their employees ('company cars') are taxed as income in the hands of the employee. Provision of company cars is relatively uncommon in Germany, but in Britain, such cars form a large proportion of all cars sold and of the total car stock. The tax treatment of company cars in the UK has been a matter of continuing controversy, partly about the extent to which tax treatment of the income-in-kind represented by company-provided cars confers a fiscal advantage on employers and employees compared with the tax treatment that would be applied to the equivalent cash income (Ashworth and Dilnot, 1987), and partly because it is suggested that company car purchasing decisions, which exert a major influence on the UK car market, tend in the direction of larger and more-polluting vehicles than would be chosen by employees if they were responsible for making car purchases out of their own income. There are potential environmental consequences of any fiscal subsidy to company cars, arising if the subsidy induces higher rates of vehicle ownership, greater mileages or the purchase of larger vehicles than in the absence of subsidy.

In Britain, the tax burden on company cars was increased sharply in the late 1980s, with the tax burden doubling in the 1988 Budget and rising by a further third in 1989. This increase in taxation of the income-in-kind that company-provided cars represent probably eliminated most of the fiscal advantage to employers and employees from remuneration in the form of a company

TABLE 7.4

Numbers of UK taxpayers receiving taxable benefits in the form of company cars and free fuel

	Thousands	
	Company cars	*Fuel*
1985–86	1,070	660
1987–88	1,550	810
1989–90	1,850	1,030
1990–91	1,950	1,010
1991–92	1,900	1,010
1992–93	1,810	910

Source: *Inland Revenue Statistics 1994.*

car rather than the equivalent income. Despite this, the number of employees receiving company cars has continued to grow, and it has begun to appear that this form of remuneration has advantages even when the potential fiscal benefit has been largely neutralised. These advantages could include the discounts available from motor manufacturers when employers purchase large numbers of cars, and the possibility that better terms may be obtained when the cars are subsequently sold if these second-hand sales are made on a large scale, rather than negotiated individually.

A further reform to the tax treatment of company cars took place in April 1994, with the aim of eliminating the distortions caused in the car market by the previous system of 'scale charges' for assessing the taxable benefit from company cars. Under the scale charge system, the taxable benefit had been based on the engine size of the car, in quite wide bands. Company car purchases had therefore tended to 'bunch' at engine sizes just below the thresholds, and there was concern that this had not only distorted the pattern of car sales, but in some cases might have encouraged individuals to seek the maximum engine size within a particular size bracket. In the system operating from

April 1994, which was introduced on a broadly revenue-neutral basis compared with the earlier regime, the taxable benefit of a company car is assessed as a direct proportion of the purchase price of the car. A taxpayer's taxable income is increased by 35 per cent of the manufacturer's list price[19] for a company car less than four years old, although a discount of one-third is available for those who drive over 2,500 miles a year on business and there is a discount of two-thirds for those whose annual business mileage exceeds 18,000. An extra one-third discount applies to company cars that are more than four years old.

The combined effect of these two reforms is to have substantially reduced the grounds for concern about the environmental impact of the fiscal regime applying to company cars in the UK. To the extent that company cars continue to be provided to employees in large numbers, this must now be largely explained in non-fiscal terms. There may well remain environmental grounds for concern about company cars — the system may link cars more closely to status than if employees buy their own cars, and this may, in turn, lead to more large cars being purchased. But the extent to which this can be traced to failings of the fiscal system is now much less than a decade ago.

Greater grounds for environmental concern do, however, remain about the taxation of free fuel provided to employees for their private use. A system of scale charges, related to engine size, continues to be used to estimate the taxable income-in-kind when employees receive free fuel from their employer for their private use. The taxation is not directly related to the amount of free fuel provided, and does not, therefore, in any way act to increase the

---

[19] Note that if companies are able to obtain discounts in bulk-purchasing of cars, the taxable income continues to reflect the list price, which is perhaps closer to the price that the employee would have had to pay if they had purchased the car out of cash income.

marginal journey cost for free-fuel users; employees receiving unrestricted free fuel face a zero marginal cost for fuel use.[20] The number of taxpayers in the UK receiving free fuel for private use is about half the total number of taxpayers with a company car — some 910,000 in 1992–93 compared with some 1,810,000 employees with a company car.

The difficulties of assessing the precise benefit from free fuel are, however, considerable. Many of those receiving free fuel for private use also drive considerable amounts in the course of business, and there is therefore a problem of distinguishing between business and private mileages. It would be necessary to rely on company records about the amount of free fuel provided, and there would be little scope for effective enforcement of the distinction between business and private fuel use.

7.4   Tax Treatment of Commuting Expenses

Unlike the UK, Germany provides tax relief for expenditures incurred by private individuals in the course of commuting to work, by allowing tax deductibility of commuting costs. This reflects a principle that employees should be able to deduct 'necessary costs to obtain, assure and maintain work' in computing their income tax liability.

The system allows a basic, lump-sum deduction in respect of commuting costs to be claimed, regardless of actual commuting costs or distances; alternatively, taxpayers can opt for a deduction based on actual commuting. Where the latter option is chosen, actual costs on public

---

[20] Employees receiving a limited amount of free fuel, less than the amount of private fuel purchases they would otherwise have made, do not experience any subsidy to *marginal* fuel use, compared with a situation where no free fuel is provided.

transport are deductible, whilst deductions for private car commuting are made on the basis of a fixed rate per kilometre.

During the 1970s, and until 1988, the rate at which tax relief for private car commuting costs was given was DM0.36 per kilometre. As Blum and Rottengatter (1990) observe, this is generally lower than the total costs per kilometre of private car use, but higher than the marginal costs. The rate per kilometre was increased in 1989 and 1990, to a new level of DM0.50 per kilometre. At the same time, however, petrol taxes were raised (from DM0.53 per litre in 1988 to DM0.65 per litre in 1989–90), thus reducing to some extent the real value of the higher tax subsidy to commuting costs through the deduction per kilometre. In addition, other changes to the income tax system had the effect of sharply increasing the distance at which the flat-rate deduction was exhausted. As a result, whilst the higher rate per kilometre increased the incentive for greater commuting by some commuters, others who previously received a distance-related subsidy through tax relief now experienced higher marginal costs, since their commuting distance was insufficient to exhaust the lump-sum allowance.[21] Blum and Rottengatter (1990) calculate that the daily commuting distance at which the system provides a subsidy to marginal commuting costs has, as a result of the reform, risen from some 8 kilometres to 19 kilometres.

There has recently been growing awareness that tax deductibility for commuting costs may encourage excessive commuting distances, or commuting using certain modes of transport — especially private cars — rather than

---

[21] Since these individuals do not receive a marginal subsidy, they face the full marginal cost of commuting decisions, so long as their commuting does not rise so much that they exhaust the lump-sum deduction.

other, less environmentally-damaging, modes. Blum and Rottengatter (1990) estimate that in 1986–87, the German tax relief for car commuters could have been responsible for additional accident costs of some DM0.9 billion per annum, and additional air pollution costs of some DM0.4 billion to DM1.1 billion per annum. Depending on the methodology used, they calculate that the tax relief cost some DM1.8 billion to DM4 billion in forgone tax revenue.

7.5 Lower Taxes on Unleaded Petrol

Both Britain and Germany have introduced a lower level of excise duty on unleaded petrol. In the UK, the lower duty on unleaded petrol was introduced in March 1987. The differential between the tax on leaded and unleaded petrol was initially 0.96 pence per litre, and has subsequently been widened; it currently stands at 4.8 pence per litre. In Germany, the duty on leaded petrol is currently DM0.10 (4.0 pence) per litre higher than that on unleaded petrol (Table 7.2).

Encouraging use of unleaded petrol by introducing a differential tax rate seems to have been relatively successful; the proportion of unleaded petrol sold has risen rapidly in many European countries. For example, in the UK, the proportion of unleaded petrol has risen from a negligible share of total petrol sales in 1986 to about half of total sales in 1993. In Germany, the market share of unleaded petrol in the Federal Republic in 1989 was some 11 per cent; by 1993, the market share of unleaded petrol across the whole of Germany had risen to more than four-fifths.

Large effects on behaviour have been achieved with relatively small tax incentives, mainly because leaded and unleaded petrol are very close substitutes. If the two varieties were perfect substitutes, even a small differential would be expected to induce consumers to switch to the lower-taxed variety. In the case of the leaded–unleaded

'Green' taxes and charges

FIGURE 7.1

Unleaded petrol: the tax differential between leaded and unleaded petrol, and unleaded petrol as a proportion of all petrol sold, UK

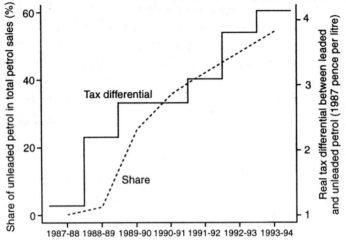

Note: Figures show excise duty differential plus VAT due on duty component.
Source: Based on data in Customs and Excise Annual Report, 1993–94.

differential, however, the rate of take-up has been complicated by the fact that only a proportion of the vehicle stock could use the unleaded fuel without modification; for some other vehicles, modification was technically feasible, although not always costless. Whilst this may have helped to reduce the rate of diffusion of unleaded petrol, diffusion rates may have been accelerated by the preference for some consumers for using the more environmentally-benign fuel.[22]

It is probably now unlikely that a higher differential would increase the take-up of unleaded petrol. In most European countries, the marginal saving when buying unleaded petrol rather than leaded petrol is already large enough to outweigh the fixed costs of converting cars to

---

[22]Tax differentiation may encourage such altruistic, 'pro-green', behaviour by signalling which goods have lowest environmental cost.

110

FIGURE 7.2

Unleaded petrol: the tax differential between leaded and unleaded petrol, and unleaded petrol as a proportion of all petrol sold, EU countries, 1993

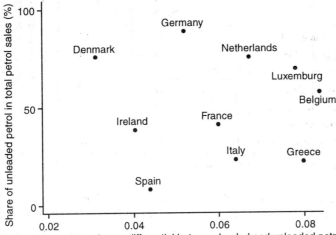

Source: Tax rates from International Energy Agency, 'Energy prices and taxes, third quarter 1993'; market shares from EUROSTAT data.

run on unleaded petrol and any efficiency disadvantage of cars running on unleaded petrol, for all except those who do very few miles per year. The remaining users of leaded fuel will contain a disproportionate number of owners of older cars, used for relatively low mileages; others may simply be poorly informed and unlikely to be responsive to marginal adjustments to the fiscal differential.

7.6 The Tax Differential between Petrol and Diesel Fuel

Whilst a tax differential between leaded and unleaded petrol has been introduced for environmental reasons in many European countries, the differential between excise levels on diesel fuel and petrol might equally be considered in the light of the environmental attributes of the two fuels. In Germany, the excise duty on diesel fuel is some

TABLE 7.5

**Percentages attributable to road transport of
UK total emissions of some pollutants, 1991**

	All road transport	Cars	Diesel-powered vehicles
Carbon monoxide	90	81	2
Sulphur dioxide	2	1	1
Black smoke	42	6	39
Nitrogen oxides	52	29	21
Fine particulate matter	27	10	16
Carbon dioxide	19	12	6
Volatile organic compounds	37	22	6

Source: QUARG, 1993, pp. 50 and 53.

43 per cent lower than that on petrol. In Britain, there had been a differential in favour of diesel fuel for a number of years, albeit smaller than the German differential. Largely for environmental reasons, however, the relative taxation of diesel was increased in the November 1994 Budget, to align the excise duty on diesel with that on unleaded petrol.

In fact, the relative environmental damage caused by petrol- and diesel-engined vehicles is complex; emissions of some pollutants, especially those affecting urban air quality, tend to be higher from diesels than from catalyst-fitted petrol cars (and in some cases than petrol cars without catalysts), whilst emissions of greenhouse gases may be rather lower. Whether diesel should be preferred to petrol on environmental grounds, or vice versa, thus depends partly on the relative weighting given to various different environmental problems.

Emissions of carbon monoxide, nitrogen oxides and total hydrocarbons are substantially lower from diesel engines than from conventional petrol engines. Figures given in QUARG (1993, p. 6) suggest that diesel-engined cars emit only some 3 per cent of the carbon monoxide emitted per kilometre by cars with conventional petrol engines, 50 per cent of the nitrogen oxides and 10 per cent of the total hydrocarbons. Three-way catalytic converters sharply reduce emissions of each of these pollutants from petrol cars. Nitrogen oxides emissions are reduced to about half the level of equivalent diesel engines, and hydrocarbons emissions to two-thirds the diesel level; on the other hand, even with a catalyst fitted, petrol cars have more than double the carbon monoxide emissions of diesels.[23]

The potential advantages of diesel engines in respect of emissions of these regulated pollutants will thus be substantially eroded by the steady diffusion of three-way catalytic converters through the petrol-engined vehicle stock; given that new cars contribute a high proportion of total mileage, the mileage-adjusted diffusion rate is likely to be rapid. In addition, diesel engines, especially when poorly adjusted, are substantial sources of emissions of black smoke and fine particulates; these are implicated in respiratory ailments, and also include known carcinogens. QUARG (1993, p. 6) observes that particulates emissions from petrol cars are so low that they are not routinely measured; particulates emissions from diesel cars 'may be an order of magnitude higher' than those from catalyst-fitted petrol cars.

Carbon dioxide emissions from motor vehicles are closely linked to the amount of fuel used and its carbon

---

[23] These figures relate to warmed-up engines. Since catalysts need time to reach their operating temperature, initial emissions levels from catalyst-fitted petrol engines can be substantially higher. The 'cold-start emissions penalty', in terms of the ratio of pollutant emissions from a cold engine to those from a warm engine, could be around 10 for carbon monoxide and hydrocarbons emissions from a catalyst-fitted petrol engine, compared with a cold-start penalty of 2 or less for standard petrol and diesel engines. When used for short journeys in urban areas, much of the advantage of catalyst-fitted engines over diesel engines in emissions of these pollutants may be lost (QUARG, 1993, p. 9).

content. Diesel engines are substantially more fuel-efficient than equivalent petrol engines; on the other hand, diesel fuel has a higher carbon content per litre than petrol. Drawing a balance between these two effects, a diesel engine needs to have an efficiency advantage of at least 11 per cent over an equivalent petrol engine for the diesel to have lower carbon dioxide emissions. Estimates given in QUARG (1993, p. 14) suggest that at a speed of about 40 miles per hour, carbon dioxide emissions from petrol cars (without catalytic converters) and diesel cars were broadly similar; carbon dioxide emissions from petrol cars fitted with three-way catalytic converters were higher, by about one-third.

The implication of the above would appear to be that the long-standing differential in favour of diesel fuel over petrol in both Britain and Germany could not be clearly justified by reference to the relative environmental damage caused by diesel- and petrol-engined vehicles. The move towards parity in the taxation of diesel and unleaded petrol in the UK reflects the lack of a convincing environmental case for the fiscal system to encourage diesel in preference to petrol. Indeed, if a high priority is given to problems of urban pollution, there would be a case to go further and to tax diesel more heavily than petrol.

In practice, of course, the differential has arisen for wholly non-environmental reasons, largely reflecting governments' concern about the impact of high diesel duties on the costs of industry. Whilst there are good reasons for motor fuels used in the course of business activity to be taxed less heavily than motor fuels used in final consumption (since, in an efficient indirect tax system, the burden of revenue-raising taxes should fall on the latter only), the distinction between diesel- and petrol-engined vehicles no longer coincides exactly with the distinction between intermediate and final consumption uses of motor fuels. The substantial differential in favour of diesel fuel in European countries has contributed to the growth of a significant market for diesel-powered passenger cars; for example, in recent years, diesels have accounted for some 20 per cent of all new car sales in the UK compared with only some 6 per cent of the existing car stock, a fiscally-induced development having some clear disadvantages from the point of view of urban air quality.

CHAPTER 8
Conclusions: Priorities for Policy

Taxes and other market incentives have the potential to reduce the economic cost of achieving a given standard of environmental protection. In comparison with existing environmental policies, which rely heavily on the administrative regulation of technologies, location and emissions levels, incentive mechanisms would allow greater flexibility in polluter responses, and provide greater scope and incentive for innovation in methods of pollution abatement. As society's demands for environmental quality grow and the range of environmental issues of concern to governments expands, the search for policy approaches that can tackle environmental problems without incurring excessive economic cost becomes increasingly important.

Despite the attractions in principle of tax incentive measures in environmental policy and the explosion of interest in their potential, practical implementation of such 'ecotaxes' has proved far from straightforward. In both Britain and Germany, actual policy measures to introduce environmental taxes have been slow in forthcoming. To date, the number of specific tax measures implemented with a primary rationale in terms of their environmental effects is very limited in each country. In the UK, indeed, the only explicit environmentally-motivated tax reforms have been to the excise duty differentials between leaded and unleaded petrol, and between petrol and diesel, although a further measure, the landfill levy announced in the Chancellor's November 1994 Budget, is under active development. Environmental tax measures in operation in Germany are barely more extensive. None the less, in both countries, a rather larger range of tax measures have been at least partly justified in environmental terms — in the UK, for example, these have included the commitment to a steady increase in petrol duty, and the extension of the standard rate of VAT to domestic energy, hitherto zero-rated.

Should the very slow progress that has been made in implementation of environmental taxes in the two countries studied in this report give us any reason to question the feasibility or the merits of 'green' taxation? Does it reflect real practical obstacles that the theoretical arguments have failed to capture? In particular, should the UK draw any negative conclusions from the fact that Germany, once in the forefront of the policy debate over environmental taxation, has made such limited progress towards translating theory into practice over the past decade?

Whilst there are undoubtedly important lessons that the UK can learn from German experience, and some surprisingly-close parallels in some of the environmental incentive policies used or under consideration in the two countries, it should be clear that there are also some important differences in the wider context of policy in Germany which have had an important influence on the introduction of environmental tax measures.

First amongst these factors specific to Germany has been the impact of German reunification. As public policy in general, and public finance policy in particular, have become absorbed with the specific issues of industrial reconstruction and legal and financial integration, this has derailed much of the impetus for greater use of environmental taxes. Much of what is currently at stake in the integration of the new Länder into German environmental policy concerns the process of adjustment of environmental policy in the east to the current practices and standards of the west; the development of new environmental taxes has appeared rather secondary to this current priority of policy. In order to finance reunification, the overall tax burden in Germany has had to rise sharply. However, as the experience of tax reform in many countries has shown, radical changes to the structure of taxation are almost impossible to implement except in the context of a falling aggregate tax burden, when the overall reduction in the level of taxation can reduce the proportion of the population who are distributional 'losers' from the new tax structure; conversely, a time when tax burdens are rising sharply is an unpromising time to attempt to persuade the public to accept new taxes. Thus whilst some of the tax rises prompted by reunification, such as the sharp rises in petrol taxes, have undoubtedly had beneficial environmental policy aspects, there has been little opportunity for more radical experimentation with new green taxes.

A second factor specific to Germany has been that provisions of the constitution concerning public finance have placed some significant constraints on the design and implementation of environmental taxes and charges. One problem, as Spengel and Wünsche (1995) have recently argued, is that the taxation of emissions would not be possible without a change in the constitution; there are also severe difficulties in introducing special levies to finance environmental spending. A second way in which the constitution of Germany affects the introduction of environmental taxes is the impact of the federal structure. In this respect, however, there are both positive and negative influences on the development of policy. Certainly, the federal structure introduces some complications; questions of jurisdiction arise, in the sense that with some types of environmental tax there is ambiguity as to which level of government is empowered to make policy, and there are also difficulties to do with the impact of tax reforms on the allocation of tax revenues between different levels of government and between different areas. On the other hand, the federal system provides considerably greater scope for policy innovation and experiment in some areas of ecotax policy; some of the tax and charge measures introduced in Germany have been initiatives taken by individual Länder and/or municipalities. In the unitary system of government in the UK, there is no scope for decentralised policy initiatives of this form.

Thirdly, it has been suggested that some of the basic principles on which German environmental policy is founded have proved an obstacle to market-based environmental policy. Historically, German environmental policy has placed considerably greater emphasis than policy in the UK on the 'precautionary' motive for policy (Vorsorgeprinzip); under this principle, action should be taken not only to control pollution that is known to cause environmental damage, but also to control pollution sources that might be liable to cause environmental damage, even where the current state of knowledge (including scientific knowledge) does not establish that damage definitely occurs. The risks of damage from pollution are unlikely to be linearly-related to the level of emissions, and the environmental consequences of excessive concentrations of pollutants are in general likely to be much less well understood than those of concentrations already encountered in practice. In these circumstances, the emphasis on 'safety' in relation to unquantifiable risks that underlies German policy may mean that there is particular reluctance to use an instrument in which the aggregate level of emissions is not directly controlled, but arises from the responses of polluters to an incentive level fixed by policy. Maintaining the current regulatory policies, by contrast, appears to offer greater certainty in pollution outcomes, and thus less exposure to the dangers that might arise if incentive measures failed to have the expected impact on polluters' behaviour.

8.1 Some Options

Chapters 4 to 7 of this report have described environmental taxes and charges in operation, or under discussion, in Britain and Germany, in four key fields: water, waste, energy and transport. In each of these areas, how far do the tax provisions in place or under discussion contribute to environmental policy objectives, and where might more be done? What, in the light of experience and analysis to date in Britain and Germany, should be included in a short list of feasible and effective environmental tax measures which might form the basis for future policy?

Water

Incentive measures could be employed to address two distinct environmental issues concerning the water system. On the one hand, incentives could be used to discourage water pollution; on the other, the price mechanism could be used to charge for water abstraction and water consumption. The environmental problems relating to pollution are perhaps rather more clear-cut than those relating to abstraction and water use, although there are certainly regions of both Britain and Germany where water resources are scarce and where a reduction in water demands would not only reduce the costs of water supply but might also have certain environmental benefits.

Incentives to reduce water pollution can be well-targeted, in that taxes or charges can be based directly on the levels of polluting emissions. Both Britain and Germany have systems of charges for water pollution based on emissions of certain pollutants, although in both cases these are not, as currently operated, ideal systems of emissions charges. In Germany, scope for the charges to have much independent incentive effect is limited by the close linkage between the liability to charge and existing regulatory requirements, and by the extensive arrangements for rebate or reduction of the charge which mean that the full rate is faced by few polluters. In the UK, the charge is simply set in order to recover costs of operating the pollution monitoring and control system, and the charge structure and level differ from what would be set if the tax were designed to operate as an environmental incentive mechanism. Nevertheless, both systems can form the basis for an evolution to more comprehensive incentive charging for water pollution; in the UK, a gradual rise in the rates, and a shift in the structure of the charge to reflect pollution damage more closely, could transform the existing administrative charges into an incentive system. In addition, there may be scope to move towards taxes more directly related to actual emissions performance, which would strengthen their environmental impact. Currently, both countries base the charge on permitted emissions rather than actual emissions. However, recent technical progress in instrumentation and measurement has almost certainly increased the number of applications where levying charges based on direct measurement of emissions would be feasible at acceptable cost.

Water charges both for abstraction and for water supply could have a role to play in reducing environmental damage through excessive abstraction in areas or at times of water shortage, and could reduce the need for water supply infrastructure, which may cause environmental damage and intrusion. In Germany, water abstraction charges have been introduced by a number of Länder, following the lead taken by the Land of Baden-Württemberg, which introduced an abstraction charge (the Wasserpfennig) based on the volume, source, and purpose of water abstraction. In the UK, charges for water abstraction are levied by the National Rivers Authority, to cover the costs of certain services provided by the NRA. As with the UK administrative charges for water pollution, the abstraction charging system could be modified to reflect more closely the social costs of water abstraction, including an element for environmental damage.

A modified system of abstraction charges could increase the cost of industrial water use and public water supply in areas where abstraction gives rise to environmental costs. Where water users pay according to use, higher abstraction charges could encourage reductions in water use and, thereby, a reduction in the environmental costs incurred through water abstraction. However, for the abstraction charge to function in this way requires that water consumers face charges related to use. Whilst this is generally true of industrial users of water, in the UK a key category of water users — households — do not, in the main, face individual incentives for water conservation. Although the proportion of water consumers who are metered has risen in recent years, well over 90 per cent of households still pay for water according to rateable value, or on some other basis unrelated to the amount of water consumed. This contrasts sharply with the situation in Germany, where volumetric charging of household consumers, based on water metering, is the rule.

Waste

Policy initiatives and proposals in both Britain and Germany are introducing a number of new market incentives relating to packaging and waste management and disposal. These include incentives both at the 'disposal' end of the waste chain and at the 'manufacturer' end.

Proposals have been formulated in both Britain and Germany for environmental tax measures on waste disposal. In Germany, a long-standing proposal for a waste charge (Abfallabgabe) seems, at present, unlikely to be implemented. In Britain, by contrast, work is underway to implement the 'landfill levy', announced in the Chancellor's November 1994 Budget. The aim of the landfill levy is principally to establish an incentive to substitute away from landfill disposal of waste to other forms of disposal or recycling and reuse. In practice, the main substitution is likely to be to incineration, which may involve lower environmental costs than landfill, especially where energy recovery allows power-station emissions of greenhouse gases to be reduced.

As with the case of water supply, there is with the landfill levy an issue about the extent to which higher costs of supply (of water, and of waste collection and disposal, respectively) should be fed through into incentives for households to reduce their demands for the service. In the absence of some form of use-related charging for household and commercial waste collection and disposal, the increased cost of landfill disposal does not feed back into incentives for reduced waste by households and businesses. Both in Britain and in Germany, the current basis for financing household garbage collection and disposal does not provide much incentive for households to minimise waste. In Germany, however, a number of Länder and individual municipalities are experimenting with alternative systems of charging for household garbage collection based on measured weight, or on other indicators of individual use. These systems would, in principle, allow the increased costs of disposal to be fed through to provide households with incentives to minimise the amount of waste requiring disposal, encouraging, for example, greater separation of waste for recycling, composting and, conceivably, changes in purchasing behaviour.

However, even with use-related charging for waste collection and disposal services, it is unlikely that clear-enough signals would be transmitted back to manufacturers and packagers to modify product design and packaging to reduce disposal costs. Packaging taxes (e.g. for drinks containers) would establish a more direct incentive for substitution away from packaging with high disposal costs. In Germany, experimentation with such taxes at the municipal level may well grow, as a result of a recent court ruling that confirmed the legality of taxes imposed by the city of Kassel on disposable packaging, cutlery and dishes for take-away food. If well designed, such taxes could reflect the environmental impact of different types of packaging and encourage substitutions both in supply and in consumer purchasing patterns that would benefit the environment.

A more dramatic impact on supply decisions is likely to arise from 'producer responsibility' measures, such as the system that Germany has introduced for product packaging and the possible systems currently under discussion in the UK. The German Verpackungsverordnung makes producers responsible for the costs of product packaging throughout its whole life cycle, including disposal costs. This responsibility has taken the form of a parallel, industry-financed, waste collection system (Duales System Deutschland), facing given targets for collection and recycling. Through this system, industrial producers face the costs of packaging disposal, and consequently face incentives to substitute towards less-costly forms of packaging. Although not a fiscal measure, the scheme has some of the incentive properties of an economic incentive system, and appears to have encouraged a considerable reduction in the amount of packaging waste generated in Germany.

Energy

Environmental taxes on energy could reflect the wide range of energy-related environmental problems. If set so as to reflect the total environmental costs of energy use, environmental taxes on energy might be set at high rates and could raise substantial revenues, enough to have an appreciable impact on the overall fiscal system. The scale of the corresponding tax burden has, however, been a major issue in the debates on energy taxes in both Britain and Germany, and much of the policy debate has been concerned with the scope for using the revenues from energy taxes to offset the industrial and distributional impact of the energy tax burden.

A carbon tax, such as the tax proposed by the European Commission, has considerable attractions as an environmental incentive mechanism; the tax rates on fuels of differing carbon content provide incentives for fuel substitution and reduced fuel use that are well-linked to the environmental effects that underlie policy. From a practical point of view, such a tax could be implemented with relatively straightforward adaptations and extensions to the existing system of fuel excises, and could therefore be administered cheaply and enforced effectively.

The Commission proposal has, however, raised concerns about the impact of the tax on industrial competitiveness, of energy-intensive industry in particular, especially if countries outside the EU do not take similar measures. In such a situation, not only would Europe's firms face a tax that competitors outside the EU would not face, but also any diversion of energy-using production to areas outside the EU ('carbon leakage') would reduce the impact of the tax on global emissions. Concerns about competitiveness have been a prominent reason for opposition to the Commission's proposal from some parts of industry in both Britain and Germany. In Germany, these objections have been part of a general unease about the cost disadvantages of production in Germany (Standort Deutschland), arising from a whole range of sources, including domestic wage rates and social and employment policies, as well as environmental obligations.[24]

---

[24] In Germany, this concern has, perhaps, been tempered by a recognition that stringent environmental policies may create employment opportunities in environmental protection and in industries at the 'leading edge' of environmental policy. 'First-movers' in environmental policy may be able to establish a technological lead in industries supplying environmental protection equipment, whilst 'followers', which enter the market too late to establish a technological lead, may become dependent on imported equipment from established suppliers in the 'first-mover' countries. Nevertheless, this argu-

Nevertheless, the problem that energy taxes would create for competitiveness can be exaggerated. In the case of most industries, the impact on competitiveness will be small, since energy is a small part of total costs. There is also scope for using the revenues from the tax to reduce other taxes that form part of business costs, just as in the case of the UK landfill levy proposal the revenues are to be used to reduce the rate of employer National Insurance contributions.

A carbon tax would raise the price of energy to industrial and household users of energy alike. If competitiveness concerns are seen as an obstacle to raising taxes on industrial energy, some reduction in energy use (albeit not necessarily the cost-minimising pattern of energy saving) could be achieved by increasing taxes on other components of energy use, such as domestic energy and petrol. As part of their programme of measures to implement the reductions in greenhouse gas emissions required as a result of the Rio conference, both Britain and Germany have made sharp increases in the tax burden on petrol. Britain also abolished zero-rating of VAT on domestic energy, although only the first phase of a two-stage rise in the rate was implemented, and VAT is now applied to domestic energy at 8 per cent. The VAT increase is likely to reduce household energy consumption, by perhaps some 3 per cent in volume terms; it has also reduced the anomaly in the relative taxation of domestic energy and of energy-efficiency materials and installation, which are taxed at the full 17.5 per cent rate. Reducing the taxation of energy-efficiency materials and installation to the energy tax rate of 8 per cent would, however, be necessary

---

ment relates to the pace of environmental policy, and even where it is accepted, there may remain concerns about the adverse impact on competitiveness if high environmental standards are implemented through taxation rather than regulation.

if the fiscal distortion against energy-saving investments is to be fully eliminated.

The abolition of zero-rate VAT on domestic energy in the UK led to considerable political protest, in part concerning the distributional impact of the tax on households, which was sharply regressive. The distributional impact of household energy taxation has been of much less significance as a political issue in Germany than in Britain, perhaps in part because of the different patterns of household energy consumption. In the UK, household spending on domestic energy is high and only very weakly-related to household incomes; the British climate and the poorly-insulated housing stock combine to give domestic energy spending the characteristics of a necessity in household budgets.

Whilst high taxes for industrial energy use may be difficult to introduce, for the reasons outlined above, there may be scope for using tax incentives in the corporate tax system to encourage greater levels of investment in energy saving. Tax incentives — such as accelerated depreciation — for investment in energy-saving technologies would be effectively subsidies paid through the tax system. As with subsidies more generally, they have some drawbacks: they may encourage excessive levels of activity in polluting industries, for example, and they require costly administrative mechanisms for assessing entitlement. Indeed, tax policy in recent years in many countries has tended to move away from using corporate tax incentives to stimulate changes in the level or pattern of investment, and in Germany, some existing accelerated depreciation measures for environmental and energy-saving investments have recently been abolished. Nevertheless, whilst there are undoubtedly difficulties in operating tax expenditures of this sort, the general presumption against use of such measures would appear less persuasive in the case of environmental investment incentives. They may, in particular, have a role where competitiveness concerns limit the level of energy taxes that can be charged to tax rates well below the 'first-best' level. In this situation, investment subsidies might be used to increase taxpayer responses to any relatively-modest energy taxes that can be introduced on industrial energy use.

Transport

There are a large number of possibilities for the taxation of transport to be modified to reflect environmental objectives, some of which have been reflected in policy in both Britain and Germany. Thus, for example, both countries have implemented sharp increases in excise taxes on petrol in recent years, with, at least in part, an environmental rationale or justification. Also, both countries have introduced a reduced rate of excise on unleaded petrol, in order to achieve environmental policy objectives. There remain, however, further possibilities for the tax treatment of transport to be adjusted to promote environmental policy objectives, including possible changes to the annual taxes on motor vehicles and to the relative tax treatment of diesel and petrol.

The environmental issues at stake in the transport field are in some respects more complex than in the other environmental policy areas that have been studied in this report. A range of environmental costs are involved, including global and local air pollution, noise pollution, and the complex aesthetic costs involved in spatial development and the construction of roads and other transport infrastructure. Some of these environmental effects are easier to identify and measure than others; for example, emissions of global pollutants from transport are comparatively easily measured, whilst the aesthetic losses from particular patterns of spatial development may be harder to define and to quantify. In addition to narrowly-defined environmental costs, however, there are further social costs associated with transport which need to be taken into account in devising the optimal pattern of public intervention. In the case of road transport, these include congestion costs and accident costs imposed on other road users, and the otherwise-uncharged costs of consumption of publicly-provided road infrastructure. If taxes or charges on road transport are to lead to an efficient pattern of individual decisions, it is desirable that all of these various social costs be reflected in the marginal costs faced by individual road users.

The complexity of the various costs involved means that most of the available fiscal policy options for transport involve some degree of approximation to the 'ideal' underlying structure of incentives. Whilst in both Britain and Germany there have been studies and technical experimentation relating to the scope for individual road-use charging, which might permit road-use charges to be levied that closely reflect individual road users' contribution to congestion, deterioration of the road infrastructure and pollution, practical implementation of such schemes seems still to be some way off. The options for current policy principally concern the taxation of motor vehicles and fuels, and the fiscal treatment of substitutes to private motoring, including public transport.

- Higher motor fuel taxes can reflect some of the pollution externalities from fuel use, especially carbon dioxide emissions, but are generally a poor approximation to other road transport externalities (congestion, accidents, uncharged infrastructure damage, etc.). Whilst short-term demand responses to fuel tax rises are relatively small, there is considerable evidence that the long-term reduction in fuel use is greater.
- Differentiation of fuel taxes can be used to reflect the different environmental attributes of various fuels. There would probably be little to be gained from widening the existing differential between leaded and unleaded petrol, since the remaining users of leaded petrol

129

are either running cars unable to use unleaded petrol or are individuals unlikely to respond to incentive measures. There do, however, appear to be strong environmental arguments for increasing the relative taxation of diesel fuel compared with petrol. Until recently, both Britain and Germany had taxed diesel fuel less heavily than petrol; whilst the differential in favour of diesel was eliminated in the UK in the last Budget, it remains in Germany. The environmental arguments would, however, justify a tax treatment that goes beyond 'neutrality' in the tax treatment of the two fuels, in the sense that, in urban traffic in particular, emissions from diesel-engined vehicles cause greater pollution damage than those from petrol vehicles, and higher taxation of diesel, per litre, would thus appear warranted.

• The system of annual taxes on motor vehicles in Germany is more differentiated according to vehicle characteristics than that in the UK, where the annual vehicle excise duty is the same for all private cars. Through its impact on vehicle ownership and scrapping decisions, the annual tax on motor cars may have an impact on the pattern of vehicle ownership and use, and higher taxation of the most-polluting types of vehicles would be likely to encourage changes at the margin, both in the types of vehicles purchased and in the scrapping of older vehicles. Graduation of vehicle excise in line with vehicle size or other characteristics of the particular model would be straightforward to introduce in the UK within the current VED system, since most of the relevant information is already held by the vehicle registration authorities. A more precisely-targeted incentive would be provided by taxes reflecting the actual emissions performance and/or recorded mileages of individual vehicles, although this would involve considerable administrative complexity and problems of enforcement compared with the current VED system.

Whilst there are tax changes that may help to ensure that individual vehicle ownership and use decisions reflect the environmental and other social costs involved, it is clear that none of the available fiscal instruments can fully reflect the complexity of the problems involved. There remains an important role for non-fiscal measures, and there is also an important role for the fiscal system to promote the availability of other elements in an integrated transport policy. In particular, where taxes cannot fully reflect environmental costs of road transport, subsidy (or low taxation) of public transport may also be warranted, since the availability of substitutes for road transport will act to increase the 'elasticity' of individual responses to the higher cost of private transport.

References

Alberini, A., Edelstein, D., Harrington, W. and McConnell, V. (1994), 'Reducing emissions from old cars: the economics of the Delaware Vehicle Retirement Program', Washington DC, Resources for the Future, Discussion Paper no. 94-27.

Andersen, M. S. (1994), *Economic Instruments and Clean Water: Why Institutions and Policy Design Matter*, OECD Public Management Service, meeting on Alternatives to Traditional Regulation, 5–6 May, PUMA/REG(94)5, Paris: Organisation for Economic Co-operation and Development.

Ashworth, M. and Dilnot, A. W. (1987), 'Company cars taxation', *Fiscal Studies*, vol. 8, no. 4, pp. 24–38.

Bach, S., Kohlhaas, M. and Praetorius, B. (1994), 'Ecological tax reform even if Germany has to go it alone', *DIW Economic Bulletin*, vol. 31, no. 7, pp. 3–10.

Barde, J.-P. and Button, K. (1990), *Transport Policy and the Environment: Six Case Studies*, London: Earthscan Publications.

Barker, T., Baylis, S. and Bryden, C. (1994), 'Achieving the Rio target: CO_2 abatement through fiscal policy in the UK', *Fiscal Studies*, vol. 15, no. 3, pp. 1–18.

Blum, W. and Rottengatter, W. (1990), 'The Federal Republic of Germany', in J.-P. Barde and K. Button (1990), *Transport Policy and the Environment: Six Case Studies*, London: Earthscan Publications.

Bond, S., Denny, K. and Devereux, M. (1992), 'Investment and the role of tax incentives', in A. Britton (ed.), *Industrial Investment as a Policy Objective*, Report Series no. 3, London: National Institute of Economic and Social Research.

Bongaerts, J. and Kraemer, A. (1989), 'Permits and effluent charges in the water pollution control policies of France, West Germany and the Netherlands', *Environmental Monitoring and Assessment*, vol. 12, pp. 127–47.

Bower, B. T., Barre, R., Kuhner, J. and Russell, C. S. (1981), *Incentives in Water Quality Management: France and the Ruhr Area*, Washington DC: Resources for the Future.

Brisson, I. (1993), 'Packaging waste and the environment: economics and policy', *Resource, Conservation and Recycling*, vol. 8, pp. 183–92.

Buchanan, J. M. (1969), 'External diseconomies, corrective taxes and market structure', *American Economic Review*, vol. 59, pp. 174–7.

References

Commission of the European Communities (1980), *Interim Report of the Special Group on the Influence of Taxation on Car Fuel Consumption*, 150/VII/80-EN, April.

— (1991), *A Community Strategy to Limit Carbon Dioxide Emissions and to Improve Energy Efficiency*, Communication from the Commission to the Council, SEC(91)1744 final.

Crawford, I., Smith, S. and Webb, S. (1993), *VAT on Domestic Energy*, Commentary no. 39, London: Institute for Fiscal Studies.

CRI (1994), *The UK Water Industry: Charges for Water Services 1994/95*, London: Centre for the Study of Regulated Industries.

Cropper, M. L. and Oates, W. E. (1992), 'Environmental economics: a survey', *Journal of Economic Literature*, vol. 30, pp. 675–740.

Department of the Environment (1993), *Externalities from Landfill and Incineration: A Study by CSERGE, Warren Spring Laboratory and EFTEC*, London: HMSO.

— (1995), *Producer Responsibility for Packaging Waste: A Consultation Paper*, London: Department of the Environment.

Ewringmann, D., Kibat, K. and Schafhausen, F. (1980), *Die Abwasserabgabe als Investitionsanreiz*, Berlin, cited in R. U. Sprenger, J. Körner, E. Paskuy and J. Wackerbauer (1994), *Das deutsche Steuer- und Abgabensystem aus umweltpolitischer Sicht — ein Analyse seiner ökologischen Wirkungen sowie der Möglichkeiten und Grenzen seiner stärkeren ökologischen Ausrichtung*, IFO Studien zur Umweltökonomie 18, Munich: IFO Institut für Wirtschaftsforschung.

Faber, M., Stephan, G. and Michaelis, P. (1988), *Umdenken in der Abfallwirtschaft: Vermeiden, Verwerten, Beseitigen*, Heidelberg.

Goodwin, P. B. (1992), 'A review of new demand elasticities with special reference to short and long run effects of price changes', *Journal of Transport Economics and Policy*, May, pp. 155–69.

Goulder, L. H. (1995), 'Environmental taxation and the double dividend: a reader's guide', *International Tax and Public Finance*, vol. 2, no. 2, pp. 157–83.

Hansmeyer, K.-H. and Schneider, H. K. (1989), *Zur Fortentwicklung der Umweltpolitik unter Marktsteuernden Aspekten*, research project for Umweltbundesamt no. 101 03 107, Cologne.

Helm, D. and Pearce, D. (1990), 'Economic policy towards the environment', *Oxford Review of Economic Policy*, vol. 6, no. 1, pp. 1–16.

Herrington, P. (1994), 'The economics of water conservation, metering and tariffs', Financial Times European Water Conference, London, 14–15 March.

HM Customs and Excise et al. (1995), *Landfill Tax: A Consultation Paper*, London: HM Customs and Excise.

'Green' taxes and charges

HMSO (1990), *This Common Inheritance: Britain's Environmental Strategy*, Cm 200, London: HMSO.

HM Treasury (1993), *Financial Statement and Budget Report ~1993–94*, London: HMSO.

Hoeller, P., Dean, A. and Nicolaisen, J. (1991), 'Macroeconomic implications of reducing greenhouse gas emissions: a survey of empirical studies', *OECD Economic Studies*, no. 16, Spring, pp. 45–78.

— and Wallin, M. (1991), 'Energy prices, taxes and carbon dioxide emissions', OECD Economics and Statistics Department, Working Paper no. 106.

Johnson, P., McKay, S. and Smith, S. (1990), *The Distributional Consequences of Environmental Taxes*, Commentary no. 23, London: Institute for Fiscal Studies.

Jüttner, H. (1990), *Umweltpolitik mit Umweltabgaben: Ein Gesamtkonzept*, Bonn: Die Grünen/Bündnis90.

Klepper, G. (1992), 'On the use of economic instruments in the environmental policy of Germany', mimeo, Kiel Institute for World Economics.

— and Michaelis, P. (1995), 'Economic incentives for packaging waste management: the Dual System in Germany', in A. Quadrio Curzo, L. Prosperetti and R. Zoboli (eds), *The Management of Municipal Solid Waste in Europe: Economic, Technological and Environmental Perspectives*, Amsterdam: North Holland.

Kolstad, C. D. (1987), 'Uniformity versus differentiation in regulating externalities', *Journal of Environmental Economics and Management*, vol. 14, pp. 386–99.

Kraemer, R. A. (1994), 'Paying for water and sewerage in Germany', *Hydrotop '91, Marseille 12-15 April 1994: Proceedings*.

— and Piotrowski, R. (1995), 'Financing urban rainwater management in Germany', *European Water Pollution Control*, vol. 5, no. 4, pp. 48–58.

Krupnick, A. J. (1986), 'Policies for controlling nitrogen dioxide in Baltimore', *Journal of Environmental Economics and Management*, vol. 13, pp. 189–97.

McKay, S., Pearson, M. and Smith, S. (1990), 'Fiscal instruments in environmental policy', *Fiscal Studies*, vol. 11, no. 4, pp. 1–20.

Michaelis, P. (1993), *Ökonomische Aspekte der Abfallgesetzgebung*, Kieler Studien 254, Tübingen: J. C. B. Mohr (Paul Siebeck).

— (1995), 'Product stewardship, waste minimisation and economic efficiency: lessons from Germany', *Journal of Environmental Planning and Management*, vol. 38, no. 2.

134

Müller-Witt, H. and Springmann, F. (1988), *Ökologischer Umbau des Steuersystems*, Berlin: Institut für Ökologische Wirtschaftsforschung GmbH, vol. 21/88.

Muzondo, T. R., Miranda, K. M. and Bovenberg, A. L. (1990), 'Public policy and the environment: a survey of the literature', International Monetary Fund, Working Paper no. WP/90/56.

Oates, W. E. and Strassmann, D. L. (1984), 'Effluent fees and market structure', *Journal of Public Economics*, vol. 24, pp. 29–46.

OECD (1989), *Economic Instruments for Environmental Protection*, Paris: Organisation for Economic Co-operation and Development.

— (1993a), *Taxation and Environment: Complementary Policies*, Paris: Organisation for Economic Co-operation and Development.

— (1993b), *Environmental Taxes in OECD Countries: A Survey*, Paris: Organisation for Economic Co-operation and Development.

— (1993c), *Applying Economic Instruments to Packaging Waste: Practical Issues for Product Charges and Deposit-Refund Systems*, OECD Environment Monograph no. 82, Paris: Organisation for Economic Co-operation and Development.

OFWAT (1995), *1995–96 Report on Tariff Structure and Charges*, Birmingham: Office of Water Services.

Owens, S., Anderson, V. and Brunskill, I. (1990), *Green Taxes: A Budget Memorandum*, London: Institute for Public Policy Research.

Pearce, D. W., Markandya, A. and Barbier, E. B. (1989), *Blueprint for a Green Economy*, London: Earthscan.

Pearson, M. and Smith, S. (1990), *Taxation and Environmental Policy: Some Initial Evidence*, Commentary no. 19, London: Institute for Fiscal Studies.

Pigou, A. C. (1920), *The Economics of Welfare*, London: Macmillan.

QUARG (1993), *Diesel Vehicle Emissions and Urban Air Quality: Second Report of the Quality of Urban Air Review Group*, Birmingham: Institute of Public and Environmental Health, University of Birmingham.

Rajah, N. and Smith, S. (1993), 'Distributional aspects of household water charges', *Fiscal Studies*, vol. 14, no. 3, pp. 86–108.

Repetto, R., Dower, R. C., Jenkins, R. and Geoghegan, J. (1992), *Green Fees: How a Tax Shift Can Work for the Environment and for the Economy*, Washington DC: World Resources Institute.

Ridley, N. (1989), *Policies against Pollution*, London: Centre for Policy Studies.

Rodi, M. (1993a), 'Tax expenditures for environmental purposes', paper presented to Seminar C (Environmental Taxes and Charges) at the annual conference of the International Fiscal Association, Florence, 6 October.

— (1993b), *Umweltsteuern — das Steuerrecht als Instrument der Umweltpolitik*, Nomos Universitätsschriften, Politik, Band 43, Baden-Baden: Nomos Verlagsgesellschaft.

Royal Commission on Environmental Pollution (1992), *Sixteenth Report: Freshwater Quality*, Cm 1966, London: HMSO.

— (1994), *Eighteenth Report: Transport and the Environment*, Cm 2674, London: HMSO.

Sandmo, A. (1976), 'Direct versus indirect Pigouvian taxation', *European Economic Review*, vol. 7, pp. 337–49.

Seskin, E. P., Anderson, R. J. and Reid, R. O. (1983), 'An empirical analysis of economic strategies for controlling air pollution', *Journal of Environmental Economics and Management*, vol. 10, pp. 112–24.

Smith, S. (1992a), 'Taxation and the environment: a survey', *Fiscal Studies*, vol. 13, no. 4, pp. 21–57.

— (1992b), 'The distributional consequences of taxes on energy and the carbon content of fuels', *European Economy*, Special Edition no. 1 (The Economics of Limiting CO_2 Emissions), pp. 241–68.

Spengel, C. and Wünsche, A. (1995), 'Umweltschutz durch Abgaben — Eine juristische und ökonomische Beurteilung von Umweltabgaben', in O. Hohmeyer (ed.), *Ökologische Steuerreform*, Baden-Baden: Nomos Verlagsgesellschaft.

Sprenger, R. U., Körner, J., Paskuy, E. and Wackerbauer, J. (1994), *Das deutsche Steuer- und Abgabensystem aus umweltpolitischer Sicht — ein Analyse seiner ökologischen Wirkungen sowie der Möglichkeiten und Grenzen seiner stärkeren ökologischen Ausrichtung*, IFO Studien zur Umweltökonomie 18, Munich: IFO Institut für Wirtschaftsforschung.

— and Pupeter, M. (1980), *Evaluierung von gesetzlichen Maßnahmen mit Auswirkungen im Unternehmensbereich, dargestellt am Beispiel der ökonomischen Auswirkungen des Abwasserabgabengesetzes auf industrielle Direkteinleiter*, Gutachten im Auftrag des Bundeskanzleramtes, Munich, cited in R. U. Sprenger, J. Körner, E. Paskuy and J. Wackerbauer (1994), *Das deutsche Steuer- und Abgabensystem aus umweltpolitischer Sicht — ein Analyse seiner ökologischen Wirkungen sowie der Möglichkeiten und Grenzen seiner stärkeren ökologischen Ausrichtung*, IFO Studien zur Umweltökonomie 18, Munich: IFO Institut für Wirtschaftsforschung.

Terkla, D. (1984), 'The efficiency value of effluent tax revenues', *Journal of Environmental Economics and Management*, vol. 11, pp. 107–23.

Teufel, D., Bauer, P., Beker, G., Gauch, E., Lenz, H., Wagner, T. and Vilja, S. (1988), *Ökosteuern als marktwirtschaftliches Instrument im Umweltschutz. Vorschläge für eine ökologische Steuerreform*, UPI Bericht, no. 9, Heidelberg: Umwelt- und Prognose-Institut.

Tietenberg, T. H. (1978), 'Spatially-differentiated air pollutant emission charges: an economic and legal analysis', *Land Economy*, vol. 54, pp. 265–77.

— (1990), 'Economic instruments for environmental regulation', *Oxford Review of Economic Policy*, vol. 6, no. 1, pp. 17–33.

Umweltbundesamt (1994), *Umweltabgaben in der Praxis. Sachstand und Perspektiven*, UBA-Texte 27/94, Berlin: Umweltbundesamt.

Vickers, J. and Yarrow, G. (1988), *Privatisation: An Economic Analysis*, Cambridge, Mass.: MIT Press.

von Weizsäcker, E.-U. (1988), 'Plädoyer für eine ökologische Steuerreform', *Scheidewege*, vol. 18, pp. 197–203.

Water Services Association et al. (1993), *The National Metering Trials Working Group: Final Report*, London: Water Services Association, Water Companies Association, Office of Water Services, WRc and Department of the Environment.